# NEVER THIRST AGAIN

## A Woman's Guide to Creative Bible Study

### DOROTHY EATON WATTS

REVIEW AND HERALD® PUBLISHING ASSOCIATION
HAGERSTOWN, MD 21740

Copyright © 1996 by
Review and Herald® Publishing Association

This book was
Edited by Gerald Wheeler
Cover design by Linda Anderson McDonald
Cover photo by PhotoDisc
Typeset: 11.5/12.5 Garamond 3

PRINTED IN U.S.A.

00 99 98 97 96          10 9 8 7 6 5 4 3 2 1

**R&H Cataloging Service**
Watts, Dorothy Eaton, 1937-
    Never thirst again: a woman's
guide to creative Bible study.

    1. Bible—Study and teaching.   2. Women in
the Bible.   I. Title.
        220.07

ISBN 0-8280-1095-1

# Contents

1

# Finding the
# Living Word

*Where are You, God?* Hannah cried out to Him at one point. *I feel myself cut off from You. I feel like a sinking boat, tossed about by a mighty tempest on the godless deep of life. . . . I can't find You, God. Do You exist? I'm not sure I believe in You anymore. There is too much evil, and I can't see You anywhere.*

God seemed to retreat further and further from Hannah during the next year. Her 5-year-old Nellie died from a bronchial infection just before Christmas. A cloud of darkness surrounded Hannah's soul, and God seemed out of reach.

The next summer, during the family vacation at the seashore, Hannah took along no book but the Bible. She determined to find God if He could be found. For several hours every day she sat in her chair on the beach and pored over the pages of her Bible.

Then one sunny day in September, while she was reading from the book of Romans, Romans 5:8 seemed to stand out in letters of fire: "While we were yet sinners, Christ died for us."

Suddenly the warmth of Christ's love surrounded her, and the reality of His presence thrilled her heart. She lay back in her chair and let His healing, comforting presence flow over her.

In recording her experience, she wrote: "After all my years of rebellion and unbelief, my Saviour still had compassion on me and has revealed Himself to me. Oh, the fullness and the freshness of His grace! . . . While I was yet a sinner, Christ died for me!"

Hannah held her Bible close to her breast as she walked back to her room. Her heart felt light. She knew she would never be the same, for she had experienced a personal encounter with Jesus Christ in His Word.

Hannah Whitall Smith, author of *The Christian's Secret of a Happy Life,* found God when she sought Him in Scripture.[1]

## THE WORD MADE FLESH

For Hannah, discovering the Word meant discovering in Scripture Jesus Christ, the Living Word, the Word made flesh.

As the *The Clear Word* puts it: "The Word of God became a man and lived among us. We saw that light with our own eyes and knew it was from God. Jesus was gracious, kind and full of light and truth" (John 1:14).

In her pursuit of the presence of God, Hannah finally found Him when she earnestly studied the Bible. Through the Written Word Jesus Christ—Immanuel, God with us in the flesh—became real to her. She found someone she could know as a personal friend.

Like Hannah, all of us, whether we understand it or not, are pursuing the presence of God. Until we find Him we will be empty, lonely, and frustrated with life, for He created us in His image and to be in relationship with Him. We are human beings made to be in a relationship with our Creator.

"[Woman], created for fellowship with God, can only in such fellowship find [her] real life and development. Created to find in God [her] highest joy, [she] can find in nothing else that which can quiet the cravings of the heart, can satisfy the hunger and thirst of the soul. [She] who with sincere and teachable spirit studies God's Word, seeking to comprehend its truths, will be brought in touch with its Author."[2]

## FINDING GOD IN SCRIPTURE

Many Christian men and women have described how they found God's presence while reading the Written Word.

George Müller, who cared for more than 10,000 orphans in England during the past century while depending only on God for their support, is known for his great faith in the power of prayer. Less well known is his equal passion for the Word of God. He wrote: "I judge that though prayer is of the utmost moment, yet still [Bible reading] is as deeply, or more deeply important than prayer itself; for when we pray to God, we speak to God; but when we read the Scriptures God speaks to us, and this is what we so much need."

He continues: "I saw more clearly than ever that the first great and primary business to which I ought to attend every day was to have my soul happy in the Lord . . . to be concerned about . . . how my inner man might be nourished. . . . Before this time my practice had been . . . to give myself to prayer after having dressed myself in the morning. Now I saw the most important thing I had to do was to give myself to the reading of the Word of God, and to meditation on it, that thus my heart . . . might be brought into experimental communion with the Lord."[3]

## RAMABAI'S SEARCH FOR GOD

Inspired by reading the autobiography of George Müller, Pandita Ramabai became a missionary to the Hindu women of India. Born a Hindu of the Brahman caste, she became disillusioned with Hinduism during her teens. She still believed in God, though she didn't know how to find Him.

Christian friends invited her to a worship service, which she found hard to understand. It puzzled her to see them kneeling, talking to their chairs. *What strange people Christians are,* she thought. *They have no gods, but pray to their chairs.*

Soon afterward her husband died of cholera, and in her grief she renewed her pursuit of God. "I felt He was teaching me," she later wrote, "and that if I was to come to Him, He must Himself draw me."

Later, while studying in England, she visited a home for fallen girls run by Christian women. "What makes you care for these girls?" Ramabai asked.

Her guide opened the Bible and read the story of Christ meeting the Samaritan woman. "Christ's love for sinners is infinite," the English woman explained. "He is the divine Saviour of the world, of all people no matter how far they have fallen."

There in Scripture, in the story of Jesus and the woman at the well, Pandita Ramabai realized that she had come face-to-face with the God she had been seeking for so long.

Describing her encounter with Christ in Scripture, she wrote: "I realized, after reading the fourth chapter of St. John's Gospel, that Christ was truly the divine Saviour He claimed to be, and no one but He could transform and uplift the downtrodden womanhood of India and of every land."

Ramabai returned to India a baptized, committed Christian. Bible study became a deep passion of her life. She learned Hebrew and Greek in order to translate the Bible into the Marathi language so that many other women could find the Living Word of God in Scripture as she had done. Starting a home for widows, she helped thousands of women find Jesus in the Word.[4]

## WAYS TO SEEK HIM IN SCRIPTURE

The ways a woman seeks God in Scripture are as varied as her experience and personality. The method is not so important as the daily effort she puts forth and the intense desire in her heart to find God.

Mary Slessor, who lived during the past century, carried her Bible with her to her work in the woolen mills and read it as much as possible during her breaks. She wrote that she felt as if God had written personally to her. Through a daily meditation on Scripture, God became real to Mary Slessor.[5]

Becky Tirabassi, author of several books on prayer, confesses that her spiritual experience was shallow and works-oriented until she started spending an hour daily pursuing God's presence in Scripture. Every day she reads a portion from the New Testament, something from the Old Testament, and a chapter from the book of Proverbs.

She meditates on the words of Scripture, listening for God's voice, finds something that speaks to her personally, then writes it down in her notebook. Through her one hour with God's Written Word every morning Becky finds the presence of the Living Word and hears Him speak to her.[6]

Lois Hall, a friend of mine from Troutdale, Oregon, once read her Bible through and shaded 20 different subjects in colored pencil. The next year she did a book-by-book Scripture search on what God is like. After praying for the Holy Spirit's guidance she wrote her own commentary on what the Bible says about God's character using no helps but the concordance and notes in her study Bible. She found the experience to be a real blessing.

One year I experimented with color coding. Using a blue pencil to underline phrases that revealed something of God's character, I was amazed at how many blue marks I had. Other colors I used were red for promises, green for commands, and purple for references to the sanctuary service. It was an exciting year of growth in my relationship with God.

Another time I focused on the different names of God in Scripture and the metaphors the Bible uses to portray a facet of His character. I had a fascinating time with that! It surprised me to see how many of the metaphors the Bible writers employed speak directly to the experience of women.

Currently I am using Dick Eastman's book *A Celebration of Praise* to guide me in a study of God's attributes in Scripture. He gives references for 60 characteristics of God. I can see that my prayer life is changing as I comprehend more and more of the awesome God who is at the same time my Friend.

WHERE ARE YOU, GOD?

Beverly Middlekauff pursued the presence of God for 50 years, but didn't find Him until the spring of 1993.

When she was a child, Beverly's parents had dropped her off at Sunday school, where she learned a lot about God, but somehow she never really met Him. Later she joined another church, became an active volunteer, took her children faithfully to Sunday school, but still felt an emptiness. Beverly visited psychics, tarot card readers, and even spent a weekend exploring the New Age movement. Still she longed for something more.

In her desire to really know God, Beverly sought out a Christian minister and asked, "Where is God?"

The pastor pointed out the window. "God is in that tree. Go into nature. You will find Him there."

Beverly bought a horse and went for long rides, seeking God, but still He seemed to elude her. *Where is He?* she wondered. *Why can't I find Him?* Then Beverly visited another pastor and asked him the same question: "Where is God?"

He shrugged his shoulders and replied, "When you find out you'll be able to write a book!"

Then in the spring of 1993 an Adventist pastor, John Glass,

moved to town and "just happened" to contact Beverly Middlekauff, a real estate agent, to help him find a place to live. After spending several days together looking at homes, Pastor Glass invited Beverly to attend his church. "I'm preaching in Minnetonka this Saturday," he said. "I'd like to invite you to attend. I think you'd enjoy it."

The timing was right. She felt her need for God more than ever now that her fiftieth birthday was approaching. Her children were in the process of leaving home, and she was facing the reality of growing older and being alone. She liked John Glass. Maybe he could help in her search for God.

After church that Saturday, Beverly approached Barbara Huff, whom she had known since 1981 when she'd assisted the Huffs in finding a house. Since then they had recommended her to several pastors on the move. "I've got to know more about your church," Beverly said. "Let's get together!"

Barbara and Beverly began regular Bible studies, and finally, there in the Word of God, Beverly met Jesus Christ, the Living Word, and accepted Him as her Saviour. She found in Him a personal friend and was thrilled.[7]

SEARCH THE WORD
## The Woman at the Well
Read the story in John 4:1-29 at least three times, preferably from three different versions.

1. Look for the following details in the story to help make the experience real for you.

a. What time of day was it? (John 4:6) (This is significant, as morning and evening were the regular times for the women to draw water. Why do you think she chose this time?)

b. What time of year was it? (December A.D. 28 or January A.D. 29. Rainy season, average temperatures 45° F to 60° F.)

c. Was Jesus sitting or standing? Why? (John 4:6) (The open well was more than 75 feet deep. A wide stone wall encircled the opening. The women could rest their waterpots on it. On this Jesus sat).

d. What containers did the woman have for water? (John 4:11, 28) (A waterpot was used to haul the water on her head,

shoulder, or hip. She would also carry a hard leather portable
bucket with a rope to draw up the water.)

   e. Where was the well located? (John 4:5) *land owned by Jacob*

   f. Where had Jesus been? (See John 4:3 and John 2:13) *Judea*

   g. Where was Jesus going? (John 4:3) *Galilee*

   h. Locate Jerusalem, Sychar, and Galilee on a map.

   i. Most Jewish travelers avoided the short route through
Samaria, preferring the longer route along the Jordan because of
the animosity between the two peoples. Why do you think Jesus
chose this route? *knew the woman would be at the well*

2. The story of the Samaritan woman illustrates seven stages
in a person's search for God. Locate the verses that speak of each.

   a. Indifference (seeming to ignore Christ's presence). *7*

   b. Doubt (startled by a Jew asking a favor of her). *9*

   c. Interest (begins to pay attention to spiritual message). *11*

   d. Conviction (conscience awakened, realizes need). *15*

   e. Evasion (focus on ceremony and doctrine).

   f. Realization (touched by Christ's character, His friendship)

   g. Revelation (recognizes Christ as the Messiah, her Saviour).

   h. Faith experience (filled with joy, shares Him with others). *29*

3. Where are you in your own spiritual journey? With which
stage of a search for God do you most identify at present?

PERSONAL DISCOVERIES

1. Read *The Desire of Ages,* chapter 19, pages 183-195. Mark
those passages that support each of the eight stages of searching as
listed in the Search the Word exercise.

2. Read the story again in the Bible. Notice how Christ reminded the woman of the written Word in order to lead her to acknowledge Him as the Living Word. Verse 10 alludes to the
following Old Testament references: Isaiah 12:3; 44:3; Jeremiah
2:13; Zechariah 13:1; 14:8. Verse 21 points to Malachi 1:11.
Verse 22 has reference to 2 Kings 17:29; Isaiah 2:3. As she focused
her mind on Scripture, she recognized Him as the Messiah.

3. Read through one Bible book, marking in blue each phrase
that reveals something of what God is like. Or choose a rainbow
of colors, each one representing a different aspect of His character.

## GROUP DISCOVERIES

1. Share with the group your own personal journey to find God. What stages did you pass through?

2. The Samaritan woman's encounter with Jesus appeared to be a coincidence, but with God nothing happens by chance. What seemingly coincidental happenings have led you to your present relationship with God? Share one with the group.

3. Brainstorm on the metaphors used to describe what God is like. Make a list of those that especially speak to the experience of women. (Examples: the Bread of Life, the Bridegroom, searching for a lost coin, a mother hen and chickens.)

---

[1] Marie Henry, *Hannah Whitall Smith* (Minneapolis: Bethany House Publishers, 1993), pp. 29-34.

[2] Ellen G. White, *Education* (Mountain View, Calif.: Pacific Press Publishing Assn., 1903), pp. 124, 125.

[3] John Steer, "Seeking First the Kingdom," *Discipleship Journal,* Jan. 1, 1996.

[4] John Woodbridge, *Ambassadors for Christ* (Chicago: Moody Bible Institute, 1994), pp. 167-173.

[5] ————, *More Than Conquerors* (Chicago: Moody Bible Institute, 1992), p. 63.

[6] Julie A. Talerico, "Becky Tirabassi: Keeping Her Balance," *Today's Christian Woman,* March/April 1992.

[7] Barbara Huff, "6,000 Miles to the Baptismal Pool," Mid-America Union *Outlook,* January 1994.

*2*

# Finding a Personal Message

On a vacation trip to the Lake District in England we visited Keswick, site of annual camp meetings during the early twentieth century. I sat on a grassy knoll overlooking a still, blue lake. Sheep grazed on quiet hillsides and swallows swooped near the water's edge. *No wonder Hannah Hurnard came here to find God!* I thought.

Nineteen-year-old Hannah had come to Keswick at the urging of her father to give God one last chance. She attended two meetings a day according to the bargain she had made with him. The rest of the time she roamed the countryside thinking.

*God, where are You? Why don't You speak to me? Maybe Christianity is all an illusion,* Hannah's heart cried out.

Friday morning there was a final meeting. However, it was different from the others. It contained no formal preaching. Twelve missionaries testified of God's power. It seemed to Hannah that their faces shone with the brightness of heaven. For three hours she sat, fascinated with the stories of God's presence in their daily struggles.

Hannah thought to herself, *There must be a God—one who is willing to speak to everyone but me. Why can't I find Him?* The testimonies ended and the leader called for all who were willing for God to use them to come forward to the front. Hundreds went forward. Hannah knew her father wanted her to respond, but she could not.

She ran from the tent to the privacy of her room and fell to her knees beside her bed. "God, if You are there, please speak to me. If You don't reveal Yourself, I shall know there is no hope anywhere in the universe."

Reaching for her Bible, she challenged the Almighty, "OK, God. Here's Your chance. Speak to me through Your Word."

The Bible fell open to 1 Kings 18. Hannah reacted in disgust. How could there be a message from God in a chapter full of strange names and evil acts? Although tempted to close the Bible, she finally decided it wouldn't hurt to read it. This was God's last chance! With little hope of finding Him, she began to read the story of Elijah challenging the false prophets of Baal. She read how God revealed Himself, consuming the sacrifice.

*God is asking me to make a sacrifice, too,* Hannah suddenly realized. *He wants me to give Him all that I have, to be willing to witness for Him, maybe even to be a missionary!*

The words of verse 21 spoke to her heart: "How long halt ye between two opinions? if the Lord be God, follow him."

After several agonizing moments, Hannah cried out, "If You will make Yourself real to me and help me, I will give You my stammering tongue, and I will become a missionary."

Opening her eyes, Hannah read the words in verse 39: "The Lord, he is the God; the Lord, he is the God." Suddenly it seemed that a warm, glorious light filled her heart. She felt two loving arms around her, and heard a voice whisper tenderly, "Here I am, Hannah. I have been here all the time, but you locked yourself away from the consciousness of My presence by refusing to yield yourself completely. Now the block is gone and you know that I am here. I love you. I will never leave you."

Hannah Hurnard had pursued God's presence in nature and in meetings, but not until she sought Him in His Written Word did she hear His voice. After that experience Hannah read God's Word eagerly, listening for His personal message. Later she wrote a book of her encounters with God called *Hinds' Feet on High Places.*[1]

We must spend time in God's Word for two fundamental reasons. The first is to find God, and the second is to discover a personal message from Him. "The Scriptures are to be received as God's Word to us. . . . In them He is speaking to us individually, speaking as directly as if we could listen to His voice."[2] God longs to communicate with us, and He does it most often through the words of Scripture.

## HOW TO HEAR GOD'S VOICE IN SCRIPTURE

1. **Pray for the guidance of the Holy Spirit.** Jesus Himself has promised that the Holy Spirit will teach us (John 14:26), speaking God's message to us personally (John 16:13). The Holy Spirit is the voice that will guide our thoughts as we read (Isa. 30:21). The Holy Spirit impresses our minds as we read the Written Word, applying to our lives just the message we need.

No wonder Ellen White suggests that "never should the Bible be studied without prayer,"[3] for "we can attain to an understanding of God's word only through the illumination of that Spirit by which the word was given."[4]

Audrey Wetherell Johnson agrees. "As any believer, after praying for the help of the Holy Spirit who lives in [her], studies the Bible, God's authority becomes real to [her]. [She] reads the Bible as God Almighty's living communication with [women]. Increasingly, the study becomes a delight, a means of guidance for life, and a direct communication of the Almighty Father who loves you and in this way makes you know His love."[5]

2. **Open your Bible and read.** Read a chapter several times until the facts are very clear. Read it in different versions. Immerse yourself in God's Word.

"Never mind if it appears dry. Read it. No matter if you think you know all about it. Read it and you will find rest to your soul, because it will point you to Jesus and lead you to His gracious feet," J. J. Ellis comments on Mary Slessor's habit of reading the Bible daily.[6]

It helps to have a plan to cover the whole Bible systematically. Some read through from Genesis to Revelation. I once read the New Testament backward, book by book, beginning with Revelation and ending with Matthew. As a result I saw things I had never seen before by attacking it in a different way.

Christine Noble, a popular women's speaker in England, reads portions from the Old Testament, the New Testament, and

Psalms/Proverbs every day. Often as she reads, God impresses her with something He wants her to do. Someone once asked her what message she would like on her tombstone. Christine replied, "She heard from God."[7]

My friend Marilyn Puccinelli is enjoying the experience of reading one chapter from each of four places in the Bible. Beginning in Genesis, Ezra, Matthew, and Acts, she reads from each part daily, but chooses to do her journaling only from the Gospels. Otherwise she figures it would be an all-day job!

3. **Think about what you have read.** Try to answer the following questions: What lesson does this passage have for me? How can I apply it to my own situation? What is God saying to me here?

Dolly MacDonald, Australian missionary to Zaire, faced a decision that needed to be made overnight. She had almost decided to turn down a particular offer when she realized she hadn't prayed about it. "All right, Lord," she prayed hastily, "what would You have me to do? I don't want to accept this offer, but I really do want to know Your will."

Then she opened her Bible to Ezra, where she had left off reading the night before. When she came to the words "Arise; for this matter belongeth unto thee. . . . Be of good courage, and do it," she knew it was the Lord speaking to her. The next morning Dolly wrote a letter accepting the offer. Later events proved her decision a wise one.[8]

I have found it absolutely amazing that the Lord is able to speak to my situation, regardless of where in the Bible I happen to be reading at the moment.

Once when I was feeling downcast because of problems in my life and in the lives of my children, the words of Isaiah 49:16 lifted me from my despair: "See, I have engraved you on the palms of my hands" (NIV).

I laid my left hand on the journal page for that day and traced around my fingers. On the palm of the hand I wrote my name and the names of my family members: Dorothy Eaton Watts, D. Ronald Watts, Selvie Esther Rupert, David Raja Watts, and Stephen Andrew Watts. Below them I wrote "God's tattoo of love! Praise the Lord!"

That experience put me on a spiritual "high" for several days.

I still feel greatly loved as I recall the personal message I received that morning long ago.

**4. Pick out a key phrase or verse.** As you read the passage, what verse seems to stand out? Read it again, underlining the part that appears to apply to you. Is it a promise or a command? I've found it meaningful to underline promises in red and commands in green.

"We should take one verse, and concentrate the mind on the task of ascertaining the thought which God has put in that verse for us," Ellen White advises us. "We should dwell upon the thought until it becomes our own, and we know 'what saith the Lord.'"[9]

After reading the story of the wedding at Cana, Audrey Wetherell Johnson asked herself *What message is God trying to give me in this story?*

To her mind came the words of Mary: "Whatsoever he saith unto you, do it" (John 2:5). Audrey asked God to tell her what He wanted her to do that day. God spoke to her quietly in her thoughts: *I want you to talk to a certain friend about Me.* She obeyed with good results.[10]

**5. Write down the message.** Eleanor Page finds it helpful to keep a notebook handy in which she jots down the impressions God gives her as she reads systematically through the Bible. For several weeks she had been praying for direction in her witness for Christ. When she came to Titus 2, verses 3 and 4 seemed to leap out of the page to catch her attention: "The aged women likewise . . . that they may teach the young women."

The Holy Spirit spoke through those verses to Eleanor. "You are the widow of a military man and have been trained in discipleship and evangelism. Who is better suited than you to share God's love with the wives of congressional and military officials in Washington, D.C.?"

After that experience in God's Word, doors began to open for Eleanor to hold Bible studies with scores of women in military and governmental circles from the White House to the Pentagon.[11]

**6. Paraphrase.** Ellen White gives an example of paraphrasing Scripture. "In His promises and warnings, Jesus means me. God so loved the world, that He gave His only-begotten Son, that *I*, by believing in Him, might not perish, but have everlasting life. The experiences related in God's Word are to be *my* experiences. Prayer and promise, precept and warning, are mine."[12]

I find it helpful to write my own paraphrase of a passage so that it applies to me and my current situation. I put my name into the verse as if God were speaking the words directly to me.

One morning began all wrong. I had a long list of to-do items, but the car was being repaired and I had no wheels. I felt out of sorts before I even dressed. In my journal I outlined my frustrations for the Lord. While I was still complaining about the impossibility of my situation, the Lord brought to mind Isaiah 26:3: "Thou wilt keep [her] in perfect peace, whose mind is stayed on thee: because [she] trusteth in thee."

I wrote this paraphrase: "Fix your mind, focus your thoughts on Me, Dorothy, for I am the source of perfect peace in your life today. It doesn't matter what comes your way to frustrate (such as not having your car when you need it). If you'll only turn to Me, I will speak peace to your heart and calm your spirit and keep it calm all day."

"Yes, Lord, I want You to do that for me," I poured out my soul on the paper. "Do it for me, please!" And of course He did!

## MICHELLE'S MESSAGE

Michelle's experience illustrates how personal God's Word can be. It was during a dark chapter of her life. She was in the hospital receiving treatment for an eating disorder. For months she had starved herself, having no desire to eat. Isolated now in her hospital room, she wondered if God cared about her problem.

Seeking answers, Michelle opened the only book she was allowed to have, her Bible. She began reading in the Psalms. Hour after hour she read, not sure what she was looking for, but longing for God to reveal Himself to her.

Then she came to Psalm 107 and felt deeply stirred as she read verses 18-20: "Their soul abhorreth all manner of meat." That's exactly how she had felt for months! "And they draw near unto the gates of death." Her doctor had explained how near death she had been. "Then they cry unto the Lord in their trouble, and he saveth them out of their distresses." Her heart beat faster as she read on. Perhaps God would save her, too. "He sent his word, and healed them, and delivered them from their destructions."

*God put those verses there for me,* Michelle thought. *This is His message of love just for me!* Although it happened many years ago, Michelle still treasures that personal word from God.[13]

SEARCH THE WORD
## God Spoke to Bible Women
Look up the texts below. What was the woman's problem? What message did God have for her?

| WOMAN | TEXT | PROBLEM | MESSAGE |
|---|---|---|---|
| 1. Eve | Gen. 3:16 | sorrow multiplied | husband rule over her |
| 2. Sarah | Gen. 18:14 | unbelief | have a son |
| 3. Hagar | Gen. 21:17, 18 | son | make a great nation |
| 4. Miriam | Num. 12:4-8 | jealous | God will speak to Moses |
| 5. Hannah | 1 Sam. 1:17 | childless | petition granted |
| 6. Mary | Luke 1:30-37 | has no man | will have a child |
| 7. Elisabeth | Luke 1:41-45 | | Mary's baby would be Jesus |
| 8. Martha | Luke 10:41,42 | frustrated | Mary has chosen God |
| 9. Mary Magdalene | John 20:17 | wanted to touch Jesus | go tell the disciples |
| 10. Woman at Well | John 4:1-42 | living with someone / not married | Jesus is the life |

PERSONAL DISCOVERIES
1. If you could spend the afternoon with one of these women, which one would you choose? Whose experience is nearest to your own? What advice do you think she would give you?

2. Try a paraphrase experiment with the book of Proverbs. (Because the book has 31 chapters, it is ideal for a month's devotional activity). Where appropriate, substitute "woman" for "man," "daughter" for "son," or put in your own name. Listen for God's message in each chapter.

3. Read through Proverbs, one chapter a day. Underline promises in red, commands in green.

GROUP DISCOVERIES
1. Share an experience about a specific verse of Scripture that was God's personal message to you. Or share your favorite Bible verse and tell why it is meaningful to you.

2. Write a number of promise texts on slips of paper. Put

them into a bowl. Let each person choose a text. While quiet music plays, ask them to meditate on the verse, paraphrasing it to meet their particular life situation. After five minutes or so, ask those who are willing to do so to share their paraphrase.

3. Divide into groups of three. Assign one of the 10 Bible women of "Search the Word" to each group. Ask them to read the story in context, then discuss the woman's problem and God's message to her. How might this same message apply to women today?

4. Pass out empty brown lunch sacks. Allow the women five minutes to find an object that reminds them of their relationship with God. Put it into the bag. Do not tell anyone. At a signal, all come together and take turns revealing their object and telling how it makes them think of God. (For instance: a comb—"God takes the tangles out of my life," soap—"He cleanses me of sin.")

[1] Isabel Anders, *Standing on High Places* (Wheaton, Ill: Tyndale House Publishers, Inc., 1994), pp. 9-16.

[2] Ellen G. White, *The Ministry of Healing* (Mountain View, Calif.: Pacific Press Publishing Assn., 1905), p. 122.

[3] ———, *Steps to Christ* (Mountain View, Calif.: Pacific Press Publishing Assn., 1956), p. 91.

[4] ———, *Testimonies for the Church* (Mountain View, Calif.: Pacific Press Publishing Assn., 1948), vol. 5, p. 703.

[5] A. Wetherell Johnson, *Created for Commitment* (Wheaton, Ill: Tyndale House Publishers, Inc., 1982), p. 345.

[6] J. J. Ellis, *Two Missionary Heroines in Africa* (Kilmarnock, Scotland: John Ritchie, Publisher).

[7] Jeff Lucas with Cleland Thom, *Friends of God* (Nottingham, England: Crossway Books, 1994), pp. 53-62.

[8] Dolly MacDonald and Hazel Fry, *Love Finds a Way* (London: Marshall Pickering, HarperCollins, 1992), pp. 68, 69.

[9] Ellen G. White, *The Desire of Ages* (Mountain View, Calif.: Pacific Press Publishing Assn., 1898), p. 390.

[10] Johnson, *Created for Commitment,* p. 345.

[11] Vonette Zachary Bright, ed., *The Greatest Lesson I've Ever Learned* (Milton Keynes, England: Word Publishing, 1993), pp. 122-127.

[12] White, *The Desire of Ages,* p. 390.

[13] Personal interview. The name has been changed to protect the woman's identity.

3

# Finding the Author's Meaning

Audrey knocked timidly on Ruth's door. Discouraged, she needed to talk to someone who would understand. Ruth Brittain, president of China Bible Seminary, seemed the right person to approach. She was a woman of experience, a true woman of the Word.

Ruth took one look at the young missionary and knew that something was amiss. "What's wrong, Audrey?"

"I'm discouraged," Audrey confessed. "Here I am in China as a missionary, but I feel so unworthy. What do I have to give these people? I need a fresh touch from God. I can't go on like this."

"Saturate yourself with God's Word," Ruth replied softly. "Go to your room and immerse yourself in one book of the Bible."

Audrey felt a little annoyed with the suggestion, though she tried not to show it. *Doesn't she realize I've just finished the Bible Institute? I know my Bible frontwards and backwards,* Audrey thought. *I've read it from cover to cover plenty of times!*

As she walked to her room, the Lord spoke to her: "Audrey, remember Naaman, who went to Elisha for a cure for leprosy. He too expected some wonderful pronouncement from the prophet. Although disappointed, just as you are now, he did as he was told, and he was blessed. Perhaps you should do as Ruth suggests."

Back in her room, Audrey went onto the balcony, opened her Bible to Hebrews, and began reading the first chapter. It seemed dry and lifeless. In desperation she looked up at the sky and cried out, "Lord, You promise that You will reward a person who truly seeks You. Please make Hebrews come alive. Speak to me, Lord!"

Beginning again, she analyzed each chapter by asking herself three questions: What does the passage say? What did it mean to the people for whom it was written? What does it mean to me?

Four hours later she had finished the whole book of Hebrews, her mind saturated with its message. Later she wrote about the experience: "It was as though God had picked me up and taken me into heaven, where He dwells. I had been with Him! My entire spiritual being was renewed. . . . Depression was gone. I had received God's words and was rejuvenated in every part of my being."[1]

## THREE BASIC PRINCIPLES FOR BIBLE STUDY

Audrey Wetherell Johnson had discovered three basic principles for understanding the Bible.

1. **It takes time to saturate yourself with God's Word.** "A casual reading of the Scriptures is not enough. We must search, and this means the doing of all the Word implies. As the miner eagerly explores the earth to discover its veins of gold, so you are to explore the Word of God for the hidden treasure."[2]

2. **We must ask for the Holy Spirit to instruct us.** Spiritual things are spiritually discerned. God has given us the Holy Spirit to teach us the meaning of God's Word. Without His guidance we can never understand what the Bible says (1 Cor. 2:10-14).

"If we would not have the Scriptures clouded to our understanding, so that the plainest truths shall not be comprehended, we must have the simplicity and faith of a little child, ready to learn, and beseeching the aid of the Holy Spirit."[3]

3. **It helps to have a study plan.** Below are five simple methods women have followed with great success: Audrey's analytical method, Ethel's enquiry plan, Roberta's discovery process, Diane's observation outline, and Fran's word study method.

## METHODS OF BIBLE STUDY

### 1. Audrey's Analytical Method

After the Communist takeover of China, Audrey began teaching the Bible to women's groups in the United States. Soon she was training people throughout the country to use three basic questions to analyze a passage of Scripture.[4]

a. What does the Bible say?

b. What did it mean to those for whom it was written?

c. What does it mean to me?

What does the Bible say? What are the facts? Who is it about? What actions happened? Where did it happen? When?

What did it mean to the people at the time it was written? What were their customs and religious beliefs? What was the background thinking behind the words used?

What does it mean to me? How can I apply this to my own situation and faith journey?

## 2. Ethel's Enquiry Plan

Ethel Herr was in the hospital for the birth of her third baby. One of her nurses told her one night, "I can honestly say that every time I open my Bible, I still get excited about what I read there. Isn't His Word marvelous?"

"Mmmmm . . . of course," Ethel mumbled. After the nurse had left, she felt ashamed of her own lack of enthusiasm. She lay awake, thinking: *It's been a long time since I could say what she said and mean it. Somewhere along the line I've lost my enthusiasm. I find the Bible dry, even boring at times. Oh, how I wish I could get excited about God's Word once more!*

The Lord rewarded Ethel's desire. During the next few months He helped her get her priorities in order so that she could spend time alone with Him and the Word. Once again she had a genuine hunger for the Bible. And once again it was alive and interesting.[5]

Ethel began leading women's Bible study groups. Eventually she wrote the book *Bible Study for Busy Women,* in which she suggests using a study worksheet with the following four basic questions:[6]

a. What does the passage say?

b. What does it mean?

c. What does it mean to me?

d. How will my life be different because I have studied this passage?

What does the passage say? Who wrote it? For whom was it written? What were the circumstances?

What does it mean? Look for repeated words and phrases that

will help to identify the theme of the passage. Watch for references to other parts of Scripture.

What does it mean to me? How does the message apply to me in my own culture and time in history?

How will my life be different? How does God want me to change my thinking or my life? How will I respond?

### 3. Roberta's Discovery Process

Roberta Hestenes wrote a book entitled *Using the Bible in Groups.* In it she describes a method that she has used with small Bible study groups for more than 25 years. The three steps she suggests are:[7]

    a. Observation

    b. Interpretation

    c. Application

**Observation.** Use a pencil to make notes of information discovered in the passage itself. Look for answers to the questions who, what, where, and when. Notice verbs used. Pay attention to repetitions, comparisons, and contrasts. Take note of the type of literature the author chose to convey the message, such as biography, history, prophecy, poetry, or letter.

Roberta suggests that this initial work with the passage is like a detective on the scene of a crime, searching for all the facts, not knowing which ones will be the clues to an understanding of the author's meaning.

**Interpretation.** Try to determine the author's meaning and purpose for writing. Read background material, look up word meanings, and read the passage in the larger context. Set down a list of questions for further research. Verify your conclusions by comparing them with other references in Scripture.

**Application.** Decide what relevance this passage has for contemporary faith and practice. What timeless truth does it have about God, people, sin, salvation, and practical godly living?

### 4. Diane's Observation Outline

Diane Forsythe, popular seminar speaker on the subject "How to Study Your Bible for Yourself," has developed a method that focuses on observation. She outlined the process in her book *Mine the Word.* It consists of three steps:[8]

    a. Survey of the whole

    b. Study of the parts
    c. Summary of the whole

Survey an entire Bible book. She suggests reading through a complete Bible book to get a feel for the whole, without paying attention to details. Note key personalities and the historical setting. What is the theme of the book, based on your surface reading? Try to write a title for each chapter of the book that briefly summarizes the thought of that chapter.

Study each chapter in detail. Read carefully this time, paying attention to word meanings and cross-references. Ask the questions who, what, when, where, and how. Go through the chapters verse by verse, mining the meaning from each verse.

Summarize what you have studied. Again write what you feel is the book's theme. Give a brief summary title for each chapter. Outline briefly the contents of each chapter.

## 5. Fran's Word Study Method

Fran Beckett enjoys focusing on a particular word, using a concordance to trace its usage from Genesis to Revelation. Joy is one of the words she examined. It was a study that took several weeks. At the conclusion she not only knew what joy means but also became a lot more joyful in the process.[9]

Joy Dawson has also found the word study method helpful. She describes an exciting time she had researching the use of the phrase "the fear of the Lord" throughout the Bible. She kept a notebook of her discoveries under the title "The Character and Ways of God." Word study became an exciting adventure in Bible study.[10]

During a period in my life when I felt both physically and spiritually weak, I focused on the promise in Isaiah 40:31: "But they that wait upon the Lord shall renew their strength; they shall mount up with wings as eagles; they shall run, and not be weary; and they shall walk, and not faint."

The Lord called my attention to the word *wait* as the condition for receiving the promised blessing. For weeks I traced the word *wait* through Scripture, meditating each day on one verse that contained it. I studied each of these references in several translations and looked up the Hebrew or Greek meanings. Next I paraphrased each of these verses as God's message to me. By the time I finished my word study, I had a much better idea of what Isaiah was trying to say.

## HELPFUL TOOLS

Just as we assemble utensils for making a cake—mixing bowl, measuring cups, spoons, electric mixer, and pans—so we need to gather some basic equipment to study God's Word. I have listed a few helpful tools below.

1. **Reference Bible.** Choose one that includes marginal references as well as maps. Some study Bibles have background information on the books as well as time lines.

2. **Concordance.** Get as complete a one as possible. It will give word meanings and all the references in which that word appears throughout the Bible.

3. **Bible dictionary.** This contains definitions of Bible topics, names of people and places, biographies, outlines of Bible books, background material, maps, and geographical notes, as well as information on culture and customs.

4. **Bible encyclopedia.** This is an expanded dictionary of the Bible that includes more detailed information on such things as climate, dress, agriculture, housing, occupations, and many other aspects of daily life in ancient times. It has drawings, diagrams, maps, charts, pictures, and calendars.

5. **Commentary.** A commentary gives one scholar's interpretation on a passage or it may give the consensus of a group of scholars. For the real joy of discovering the Bible message for yourself, you should consult it only after you have done your basic study, made your own notes, and come to your own conclusions. Then it can be helpful to compare your conclusions with those of the commentators, revising your ideas as the commentary appears helpful.

## SEARCH THE WORD

### Mary, the Bible Student

It is evident that Mary was not illiterate. She knew the Hebrew scriptures well. We see evidence of this in the illusions to Old Testament passages in her hymn of praise in Luke 1. References from the Old Testament appear in Gabriel's message in Luke 1. Obviously he expected her to understand his illusions to the stories of other people who had been visited by angels, as well as to the prophecies of the Messiah's coming.

Read the marginal references for the following verses to gain an appreciation for Mary as a Bible student. Make a chart that lists phrases from Luke 1, and beside each phrase write the comparable phrase from the Old Testament reference.

1. The Angel's Message to Mary (Luke 1:26-38)
   a. Verse 28: (Dan. 9:23; 10:19; Judges 6:12)
   b. Verse 31: (Isa. 7:14)
   c. Verse 32: (Ps. 132:11; Isa. 9:6, 7; 16:5; Jer. 23:5)
   d. Verse 33: (Dan. 2:44; Micah 4:7)
   e. Verse 37: (Gen. 18:14; Jer. 32:17)
2. Mary's Song of Praise (Luke 1:46-55)
   a. Verse 46: (1 Sam. 2:1; Ps. 34:2, 3)
   b. Verse 48: (1 Sam. 1:11; Ps. 138:6)
   c. Verse 49: (Ps. 71:19; 126:2, 3; 111:9)
   d. Verse 50: (Gen. 17:7; Ex. 20:6; Ps. 103:17)
   e. Verse 51: (Ps. 98:1; 118:15; Isa. 40:10; Isa. 33:10)
   f. Verse 52: (1 Sam. 2:5; Ps. 34:10)
   g. Verse 54: (Ps. 98:3; Jer. 31:3)
   h. Verse 55: (Gen. 17:19; Ps. 132:11)

## PERSONAL DISCOVERIES

1. The angel referred to three other individuals in Bible history visited by angels. Who were they? (See references for verses 28 and 37.) The predictions of which prophets did the angel say were being fulfilled through Mary? (See verses 31-33.)

2. Divide a sheet of paper into two vertical sections. Label one Hannah's Song (1 Samuel 2), the other Mary's Song (Luke 1). Compare the two songs, writing the phrases that are similar side by side. Compare and contrast the two women's experiences.

3. Read through all of 1 John. Circle each action verb. List the 10 action verbs that give instructions about how Christians are to behave. Write a summary statement for each action.

## GROUP DISCOVERIES

1. Which of the five Bible study methods have you tried? Share your experience. Which of the five Bible study methods appeals to you most? Why? Which seems easiest? Which appears hardest?

2. Do a word study on one of the fruits of the Spirit as listed in Galatians 5:22, 23. Using a concordance, choose several texts

employing that word. Write each text on a slip of paper and put it in a bowl. Let each group member choose one or two texts to look up and meditate on for two or three minutes. Then let each share her text and her thoughts.

3. Divide into groups of four or five. Assign each group one of the following psalms: 1, 8, 14, 24, 46, or 67. Let the groups work for five minutes, pooling their ideas of a title for their psalm. Form a consensus about the title the group likes best. Call the groups back together to read their psalm and give their title.

---

[1] A. W. Johnson, *Created for Commitment,* pp. 110-113.

[2] Ellen G. White, *Fundamentals of Christian Education* (Nashville: Southern Publishing Assn., 1923), p. 307.

[3] ———, *Testimonies for the Church,* vol. 5, p. 703.

[4] Johnson, pp. 43, 200, 201.

[5] Ethel L. Herr, *Bible Study for Busy Women* (Chicago: Moody Press, 1983), p. 17.

[6] *Ibid.,* pp. 60, 61.

[7] Roberta Hestenes, *Using the Bible in Groups* (Philadelphia: Westminster Press, 1985), pp. 57-60.

[8] Diane Forsythe, *Mine the Word* (College Place, Wash.: BoDi Development Systems, 1982), pp. 89, 147-151.

[9] Lucas with Thom, *Friends of God,* pp. 111-117.

[10] V. Z. Bright, ed., *The Greatest Lesson I've Ever Learned,* pp. 65-70.

4

# Finding Real People

One hundred women stood at attention in Ravensbruck concentration camp, the predawn chill causing them to shiver in their flimsy clothing. From a building nearby came sounds of blows falling in regular rhythm punctuated by the screams of women. Trembling hands at her side, Corrie ten Boom longed to press them against her ears to shut out the sound, but knew that her own guards were watching.

*Lord, how long must we endure this inhumanity?* Corrie thought. *How much misery can we take?*

The instant the guards dismissed them, the women rushed to the door of Barracks 8. Once inside, Corrie went to the bed she shared with her sister Betsie and three other women. Betsie opened her Bible and began to read.

A group of women gathered. Corrie compared them to "waifs clustered around a blazing fire," holding out their hearts "to its warmth and its light." They leaned toward Betsie, eyes focused on her as she softly read. Their faces glowed as the stories came alive for each of them.

Corrie wrote, "It was new; it had just been written. I marveled sometimes that the ink was dry. . . . I had read a thousand times the story of Jesus' arrest—how soldiers had slapped Him, laughed at Him, flogged Him. Now such happenings had faces and voices."[1]

Every Friday at Ravensbruck the women had to strip naked

and line up in the unheated hospital hall for medical inspection. It was humiliating to file past leering guards. *If only I could cover myself with my hands,* Corrie thought. But she didn't dare.

On one of those Fridays Corrie stood in line behind her sister Betsie. As she saw the blue-splotched skin of her sister's bare back, the sharp lines of her shoulder blades, and the goose bumps on her spindly arms, she felt her sister's shame and longed to cover her. Suddenly the story of the Crucifixion came alive for Corrie.

*That's how Jesus was at Calvary!* she realized with a sudden burst of insight. *They took all of His clothes, too. He hung naked on that cross. He too was exposed to the scornful grin of His persecutors! He knows how we feel!*[2]

## REAL FACES AND VOICES

Are the people in the Bible stories as real to you as they were to Corrie and her sister Betsie? Do they seem as real as the woman next door with whom you share a frosty glass of lemonade on a sweltering day? Can you imagine yourself swapping camping stories with Sarah or Zipporah? Can you picture yourself talking over parenting problems with Eve? Can you see yourself sitting across the table from Hannah sharing your longing to have a child? Or can you visualize yourself grieving with Rebekah over a child that has gone far from home?

How can we become better acquainted with Bible people? I'll share a few ideas from my own experience that made the Bible characters come alive for me.

## HOW TO STUDY BIBLE BIOGRAPHIES

Soon after my decision to keep a spiritual journal I decided to do a study of Bible women. I chose to begin with Mary and Martha, the sisters of Lazarus. Here are some things I did.

1. **I wrote down my discoveries.** I have a file now of several pages of what I learned about these women. Having a pencil and a piece of paper near at hand is invaluable in getting acquainted with Bible people. "The simple act of recording also becomes an effective means of concentration and thus helps you to avoid being superficial," points out Leo R. Van Dolson.[3] Irving L. Jensen, of Moody Bible Institute, agrees. "As far as the mental abilities are

concerned, nothing crystallizes or makes permanent or helps one's remembering, as does writing down the things studied."[4]

**2. I gathered the facts.** I began by writing down all the references that told about Mary and Martha. As I read each of them I recorded the basic facts that I learned, something like what you would do in a résumé. I included facts about their family, relatives, hometown, occupations, background, and experiences. I read the stories in several translations. Next I read what Ellen White wrote about them in *The Desire of Ages*. Then I looked them up in a Bible dictionary and a book I have about all the women of the Bible. Finally I read *The Seventh-day Adventist Bible Commentary* notes.

**3. I focused on the five senses.** Using my imagination, I pictured each scene, listing everything I could see, hear, feel, taste, or smell. I tried to be specific and descriptive.

**4. I did background research.** Looking for facts that are not given, but are implied because of where and when they lived, I jotted down questions I had about the place they lived, the time of year the stories happened, the geography, the climate, and the manners and customs of those times. To answer these questions I turned to a Bible encyclopedia for charts about the climate. Then I read about such things as how people dressed, slept, cooked, and ate in New Testament times. I wanted to find out what the houses looked like. What were the burial customs of their day? What might the countryside have been like around Bethany?

After making a sketch of a house Mary and Martha might have lived in, I began to be able to see the room where Mary sat at Christ's feet. My research enabled me to visualize the kitchen where Martha worked. I could imagine the feast at Simon's house and could smell the steaming food.

**5. I studied personality and character.** Listing Mary's and Martha's character strengths and weaknesses, I compared them with a list of temperament strengths and weaknesses I had found in a book by Florence Littauer, *Your Personality Tree.*

Eventually I decided that Mary was very much a people person, easily swayed by others, a devoted friend, a good listener, sensitive to the needs of others, and sensitive to the criticism of her peers. I wondered if maybe she was phlegmatic in temperament. Martha was organized, a hard worker, a worrier, a doer, a take-charge woman, one who got frustrated when people didn't follow her directions. I could see that Martha had many of my own choleric strengths and weaknesses.

**6. I focused on the feelings.** I tried putting myself in the place of these sisters in each incident. How did they feel? What factors were causing them to respond that way? How would I have felt had I been in their shoes?

As I remembered times when someone I had depended on didn't show up, I could empathize with Martha's frustration in the kitchen. On the other hand, I thought of how neat it was to have a mother and father who listened to me by the hour when I came home from boarding school. That sharing of our lives was more important to me than the food on the table, for it fed my soul. Such memories helped me understand something of Mary's heart.

**7. I looked at problems and solutions.** What difficulties did these women have to face? What temptations did they have to overcome? What did Jesus do for each of these women? How did He solve their problems or meet their needs?

**8. I focused on God's character.** How did Jesus interact with these women? What does His interaction teach me about His character and what He wants to do in my life?

### BIBLE BIOGRAPHIES ARE DIFFERENT

As people in Scripture became real people, not just characters in a story, I found that Jesus also became more real to me. I began to understand that this is because the biographies in the Bible are very different from those on my library shelves.

Ethel Herr suggests five ways that Bible biographies differ from secular biographies: they are incomplete; pieces of the biographies are often scattered throughout the Bible; incidents do not appear in chronological order; God, not the human being, is the main character in all Bible stories; and Bible biographies represent God's point of view.[5]

**1. Bible biographies are incomplete.** Inspiration did not intend to give the story of that person's life, but rather to present him or her as just a part of God's biography. The incidents do not seek to satisfy our curiosity, but to teach us something about God.

**2. God, not the human being, is the main character in all**

Bible stories. For this reason the biblical author presents only those details that reveal God's purpose. Inspiration offers the incidents not to exalt that person's achievements, but rather to show God's accomplishments. The writer will often reveal unflattering facts about the human being because it helps to highlight an aspect of God's character.

3. **Pieces of the biography are scattered throughout the Bible.** It takes some detective work to pull all of the known parts together to get a picture of the whole. You may have to check the concordance to track down all references to a certain person. Marginal references may lead to other places that mention the experience.

4. **Incidents do not always appear in chronological order.** The focus is on God's working in a person's life, not on the order in which things happened.

5. **Bible biographies represent God's point of view.**

"These biographies differ from all others in that they are absolutely true to life. It is impossible for any finite mind to interpret rightly, in all things, the workings of another. None but He who reads the heart, who discerns the secret springs of motive and action, can with absolute truth delineate character, or give a faithful picture of a human life. In God's Word alone is found such delineation," writes Ellen White.[6]

Only God can view a person's life from the perspective of eternity. Each biography included in Scripture has a reason for being there—it teaches something God wants us to learn.

### Why Study Bible Biographies?

"Now all these things happened to them as examples, and they were written for our admonition, upon whom the ends of the ages have come," declares Paul (1 Cor. 10:11, NKJV).

God is constantly at work revealing Himself in the lives of human beings. By relating to Bible characters as real people, living in real places, facing real problems, we better understand how God can work in our own lives. This was certainly true of Pauline Hillier.

### Pauline's Pursuit

God was only a word that Pauline Hillier had heard, one that she had wondered about. Her father was an atheist. No one discussed the

Bible in Pauline's home except in mockery. Yet Pauline had still heard of God and wondered if He really did exist.

One day Charles Forrester, a new pastor in town, came to call at the Hillier home. No one had warned him that he would be unwelcome there. It so happened that the day he called, Mr. Hillier was away on business and Mrs. Hillier was taking a nap. Pauline answered the door.

*This is my chance!* the girl thought. *I must make sure we are not interrupted.* She excused herself for a moment and hid her mother's clothes just in case she awoke before the visit ended. Returning to the living room, Pauline sat down across from the pastor. She wasted no time in getting to the point.

"You must tell me whether or not there is a God," she blurted out. "Because, if there is not, I don't wish to go on living."

"Most certainly there is a God!" Pastor Forrester assured her. "He cares about you very much."

"I'm so frustrated with life," the girl admitted. "It has all seemed so pointless. I have no hope for the future."

"God has a plan for your life," the pastor continued. "He died long ago to give you hope. He has a bright future for you."

"I want to believe," Pauline said. "But I don't know how."

"A man in the Bible once fell at Jesus' feet and prayed 'Lord, I believe. Help my unbelief.' You can pray the same prayer. God will help you believe," the minister said with conviction.

For seven months Pauline prayed that prayer every day: "Lord, I believe. Help my unbelief." Still she could not find God.

Then one day she climbed into the attic to look for a toy she had enjoyed as a child. She couldn't find the toy, but she did find a Bible. It had her name on it.

*Someone must have given it as a gift,* Pauline reasoned, *and my parents hid it up here so I wouldn't read it. But now that I have found it I will read it for myself to see what it has to say about God.* She hid the small Bible in the folds of her clothes and took it to her room.

That night when she was certain all were asleep, Pauline read Mark's Gospel by candlelight. She couldn't put it down. The stories were so real, so gripping! When she came to the story of the soldiers hammering nails through Jesus' flesh, she stopped reading a moment and looked at her own hands.

There Pauline saw the scar made by a screwdriver many years before. The injury had hurt intensely. She saw again the blood flowing from the wound, felt again the pain of the puncture. The girl remembered how it had throbbed for a long time until it finally healed.

Suddenly Pauline knew that the wounds of Jesus were just as real as her own. Truly a living God, He had suffered and died for her! He was alive and wanted to be her friend! Through the stories of Scripture she had come face-to-face with the Star of all the stories, Jesus Christ, the Son of God.[7]

SEARCH THE WORD

### Ruth's Résumé

References: The book of Ruth; Matthew 1:5; *The Seventh-day Adventist Bible Commentary,* vol. 2, pp. 423-444.

1. Name: Ruth
2. Address: first marriage; second marriage
3. Nationality:
4. Religion: childhood; first marriage; second marriage
5. Husband and children: first marriage; second marriage
6. Dates for her story:
7. Other biblical characters living about this time:
8. Occupations:
9. Make a list of 10 important events in Ruth's life

PERSONAL DISCOVERIES

1. Do a character study on Ruth. List personality strengths and weaknesses. Does she seem to you to be more sanguine, choleric, melancholy, or phlegmatic in temperament? You may want to do a similar study on Naomi. How do they compare?

2. Put yourself in Ruth's place at each of the 10 major events in her life that you listed above. What feelings do you think she was having during each event?

3. Read Ruth 2:1-17 about gleaning in the field of Boaz. Imagine that you were there that day. What would Ruth have seen? What would she have felt, tasted, and smelled?

4. What does the story reveal about the character of God? How can I identify with Ruth? What message does God have for me?

GROUP DISCOVERIES

1. Make a list together of well-known Bible women. Discuss the following questions: a. Which one would you want on a nominating committee? Why? b. Which one would you like to sit beside on an airplane flight? What would you discuss? c. With which one would you feel most comfortable sharing your personal life story?

2. What Bible woman would you nominate for "Woman of the Year" in the following categories: community service, church leadership, parenting, outstanding accomplishment, professional achievement, and civic responsibility? Support your nomination with reasons. Are there other categories you would like to include?

---

[1] Corrie ten Boom, *The Hiding Place* (Carmel, N.Y.: *Guideposts,* 1971), pp. 177, 178.

[2] *Ibid..*, pp. 178, 179.

[3] Leo R. Van Dolson, *Hidden No Longer* (Boise, Idaho: Pacific Press, 1968), p. 34.

[4] Irving L. Jensen, *Independent Bible Study* (Chicago: Moody Bible Institute, 1963), p. 17.

[5] E. L. Herr, *Bible Study for Busy Women,* pp. 133-140.

[6] E. G. White, *Education,* p. 146.

[7] Irene Howat, ed., *Light in the Middle of the Tunnel* (Fern, Scotland: Christian Focus Publications, 1994), pp. 47-59.

5

# For Physical Needs

Kathy Bartalsky sat at the kitchen table, her head in her hands, staring at the stack of bills piled up before her—13 of them. *There's no way I can pay all of these bills and write a check for tithe, too,* she thought. *Lord, what am I going to do?*

Staring out the window, she remembered the pledge she and Steve had made to start paying tithe. The words of Malachi 3 came to mind: " 'Will a man rob God?' . . . 'Bring the whole tithe into the storehouse.' . . . 'Test me in this,' says the Lord Almighty" (verses 8-10, NIV).

"Lord, You are going to have to do this," Kathy said, taking another look at the bills. She opened the checkbook, picked up her pen, and wrote out the tithe check first.

Kathy later described what happened next: "I wrote check after check, and when I was finally through, we were left with about $5 in our account. Our cupboards had food, we had clothes and a home. God was faithful to supply for all our needs." [1]

Kathy Bartalsky knows we can depend on God to meet all of our physical needs. He does what He says He will do (see Num. 23:19). Let's look at some of the promises Christian women have depended on for their physical needs.

FOOD: PSALM 34:10

"The young lions do lack, and suffer hunger: but they that

seek the Lord shall not want any good thing."

During the Great Depression of the 1930s Lillian Thrasher was the director of an orphanage in Egypt. When American support dwindled, Lillian went around the countryside on a donkey looking for scraps of food for her children.

"I can't do this anymore, Lord," she cried one morning. Then, drying her tears, she knelt by a chair and prayed, "I'll take care of the children, Lord. You provide the money. I've no strength to beg and then to care for the children too. I'm depending on You!"

That week 40 more homeless, hungry children arrived. She accepted them all, but wrote to a friend, "Can you imagine what it means for me to have the responsibility for seeing that two thousand meals are provided daily as well as books, clothes, and the other needs of hundreds of children?"

During those years Lillian never had the money for food even one day in advance, but she trusted God to supply, and He did! When the Depression years ended, Lillian wrote, "God has never failed me all these years; we are fed like the sparrows which have no barns or storerooms."[2]

Amy Carmichael was a woman of faith who founded Dohnavur Fellowship in southern India. Caring for rescued temple prostitutes, she depended completely on the promises of the Word. She never made an appeal for funds, nor would she allow anyone else to solicit on their behalf. Carmichael told of their needs only to God, and of course God was faithful to supply them.

In 1950, after nearly a half century at Dohnavur, her family consisted of nearly 1,000 people, including rescued women, children, and volunteer workers from India and Europe. The organization had nurseries, dormitories, bungalows, storerooms, workrooms, classrooms, farm and pasturelands, gardens, and a hospital. I visited Dohnavur Fellowship in 1981, and it still carried on its work depending solely on God's promises.

Amy wrote several books about the amazing way that "the God who could provide food for a prophet through the instrumentality of ravens and a poor widow was trusted to meet the daily needs of children and those who cared for them."[3]

## CLOTHING: MATTHEW 6:30

"Wherefore, if God so clothe the grass of the field, which today is, and tomorrow is cast into the oven, shall he not much more clothe you, O ye of little faith?"

I well remember the day when I reminded God of this promise. We were living in Saskatoon, Saskatchewan. My husband was a young pastor and I had no job. I barely had money for panty hose, let alone a new dress.

Ron found me that morning sitting on our bed, crying. "What's wrong?" he asked, putting an arm around my shoulders.

"I have nothing to wear that fits me!" I wailed. I held up a Sabbath dress for him to see.

He chuckled. "Well, the Lord has surely looked after us well!" he quipped. "It doesn't look as if you've been starving!" I didn't think it was funny.

When Ron left, I knelt beside my bed and prayed, "Dear God, please, I need a Sabbath dress that fits. You have promised to supply all our needs, and this one is urgent!"

I heard no audible voice, but I did receive a definite impression that I should go to town and buy a dress. "But Lord, I have no money!"

"Come on, Dorothy; let's go!" I could almost hear the Lord say. "You leave the money to Me. You can depend on My Word."

So I got dressed, caught the next bus, and found myself walking down the street window shopping. I hadn't gone a full block when I met a friend. "What are you doing here?" she asked.

"I'm looking for a Sabbath dress."

"Now, isn't that interesting?" she beamed. "I have just come down to buy you a gift and was wondering what to buy!"

We chose a classic black dress with a detachable white collar that I wore for the next 10 years. Each time I wore it I thought of the day I depended on God's Word to supply me with clothing.

## SHELTER: PHILIPPIANS 4:19

"But my God shall supply all your need according to his riches in glory by Christ Jesus."

Edith Schaeffer burst into tears when the landlord told her the monthly rental price for the house she had just seen. The sum was more than they had been paying for a year in their previous home.

As Edith walked slowly away from that house, she thought about the bind her family was in. They had been evicted. Two of her four children were sick. Either they found something that day or they had to leave Switzerland and abandon the mission God had given them, yet there were no houses to be had. The one she had just looked at was the only one for rent, and it was too expensive.

Edith's mind turned to the promises of Scripture. Remembering the miracles God had performed to supply the needs of Elijah, Daniel, and Joseph, she felt a surge of faith. "God, if You want us to stay in Switzerland," she prayed, "I know You are able to find a house and lead me to it in the next half hour. Nothing is impossible to You."

Her eyes still red from weeping, Edith reached the main street of Villars just as a crowd of happy skiers returned from their day on the slopes. She hoped she wouldn't meet anyone she knew.

"Madam Schaeffer, have you found a house yet?" someone called.

Looking up, she saw a real estate agent she had approached several days before. He had had nothing to show in their price range.

"No," Edith replied.

"I've found an empty chalet," he said. He took her to the village of Huemoz and showed her the house that later became the home of L'Abri Fellowship.

There was only one problem. It was for sale, not for rent. She agreed to meet the agent the next morning with her husband, Francis, although she knew they couldn't afford it. Yet she felt convinced that God was providing that house.

At home that night she prayed for an hour. Suddenly, she says, "I was flooded with assurance that nothing is impossible to God." Next she prayed, "Lord, if we are to buy this house, send us $1,000 before 10:00 tomorrow morning."

The following morning the mail carrier delivered three letters to the Schaeffers. One contained a check for $1,000 from a couple in Ohio with the stipulation that it be used to "buy a house somewhere that will always be open to young people."

Not only did God send that check, but He also helped them meet all their payments on time. Edith Schaeffer knows that you can depend on the Word of God![4]

40

## MONEY: MATTHEW 6:8

"Your Father knoweth what things ye have need of, before ye ask him."

When Audrey Wetherell Johnson was enrolled at the China Inland Mission (now Overseas Mission Fellowship) Training Institute in England, one of the principles she learned there was to depend on God completely to meet all her needs. Sometimes she was so short of money that she didn't have enough for a postage stamp. However, when she prayed, claiming Bible promises, God always provided.

One morning as she was dressing she noticed that she had worn holes right through the soles of her shoes. She voiced her concern as she put them on, "Look, Father, I've worn through my shoes." In less than an hour a friend invited her to her room. A box of clothes had just arrived. The friend picked up a pair of shoes, "These are too big for me. Could you use them?" They fit exactly!

On another occasion Audrey had to attend a mission conference in another city. The institute required all the students to go, but she had no money for the ticket. Claiming God's promises, she went to the London train station.

Audrey was praying hard as she joined the long line before the ticket window. "Lord, if I'm to go to that conference, You'll have to work fast!" The line grew shorter. Soon it would be Audrey's turn and her pockets were empty.

Just then one of the other girls came over to her and said, "Audrey, all this week I've been impressed to give you some money." She pressed some bills into Audrey's pocket.

Quickly Audrey told her story, then stepped up to purchase her round-trip ticket to the conference. Even before she had asked, God had been impressing her friend! Audrey knows you can depend on the Word to meet all your needs—even postage stamps, shoes, and train tickets![5]


## VITAMINS: PSALM 84:11

"No good thing will he withhold from them that walk uprightly."

I have read Corrie ten Boom's *The Hiding Place* through twice. Also, I've visited the Ten Boom house in Haarlem, Netherlands, and listened to a guide tell the story of her life. Each time I've reviewed her story I've been amazed at how much the Bible meant to her and how much she depended on the Lord to meet all her needs.

I love the story about the vitamin drops. She had smuggled a small bottle of them into the prisoner-of-war camp to help her sister Betsie, who was not well.

At one point Betsie was desperately ill, and the small bottle of drops was the only medicine Corrie had that would help. Of course, many others were sick and needed it just as much as her sister.

Miraculously, Corrie always had enough drops for those in need. Somedays she gave drops to 15 or 20 women burning with fever, but when she tipped the bottle for Betsie there was always another drop or two. The bottle was dark and Corrie couldn't see how much was left, but she simply prayed and asked God to let it last as long as needed.

That bottle of medicine seemed to go on and on like the widow of Zarephath's cruse of oil. "I don't understand it!" Corrie told her sister one night as they lay on the rough straw in the dark.

"Don't try too hard to explain it, Corrie," Betsie laughed softly. "Just accept it as a surprise from a Father who loves you."

At last Corrie got a sympathetic guard to get more vitamins for her. When they arrived she took out the old vitamin bottle to finish it first, not wanting to waste even one drop. To her amazement, the old bottle was empty! Not one drop remained. God had been faithful in meeting each day's need for vitamins until more arrived.[6]

"Nothing that in any way concerns our peace is too small for Him to notice"[7]—even postage stamps, train tickets, or vitamin drops! God has "a thousand ways to provide for us, of which we know nothing."[8] We can depend on the Word!

SEARCH THE WORD
### The Widow of Zarephath

References: 1 Kings 17; Luke 4:25, 26; Hebrews 11:35; *Prophets and Kings,* pp. 129-132.

1. WHO are the characters in this story? Write down all the facts you can find about each one.

2. WHERE did the miracles in this story take place? Locate them on a map of Old Testament times. In what country was each?

How far was it between the Cherith and Zarephath?

   3. WHAT happened in this chapter?

      a. List the times Scripture mentions "the word of the Lord." Underline the phrases.

      b. List the promises God gave to Elijah and to the widow.

      c. List the miracles that occurred.

      d. List everything you might see, hear, smell, taste, and feel.

      e. What feelings might the widow have experienced during different parts of this story?

   4. WHEN did these miracles occur? (date, time period)

   5. WHY was this widow the only one to whom God sent Elijah during the famine? (See Luke 4, Hebrews 11, and *Prophets and Kings*.)

   6. HOW does this story apply to my life?

## PERSONAL DISCOVERIES

   1. Write the story of the widow's miracles from her point of view, as if she were telling the story to a friend, or perhaps to her son when he has grown.

   2. Four scenes appear in this chapter: verse 1; verses 2-7; verses 8-16; and verses 17-24. Choose a brief title for each.

   3. Select one of the promises given in this chapter. Plan a creative art or craft project to depict it. (Ideas: needlepoint, cross-stitch, glass painting, calligraphy, poster, felt banner, bookmark, liquid embroidery, collage, diorama, table arrangement, bulletin board, greeting card, quilt.)

## GROUP DISCOVERIES

   1. Ask the women to share incidents when God kept His promises to supply their physical needs. It may have been for food, shelter, clothing, medicine, money, transportation, a job, or any other tangible temporal need.

   2. Have the women read through Hebrews 11, paying special attention to any women mentioned. Name them. No name is actually given for two of them. What physical needs did God supply for each woman?

3. Provide paper, cardboard, and sketching materials such as pencils, crayons, colored markers, or chalk. Ask the women to choose one of the five promises discussed in this chapter. They are to spend 10 to 15 minutes making a poster or sketch to illustrate one of the promises. Afterward, put the sketches on display. Can the others guess which text they chose?

4. If you were preparing the story of the widow of Zarephath with the hopes of making it a best-seller in the marketplace, what title would you give your book? Try to think of a title that would cause secular women to want to read the book. What picture would you put on the cover?

[1] Kathy Bartalsky, *Soaring on Broken Wings* (Kent, England: OM Publishing, 1990), pp. 72-75.

[2] Harold Ivan Smith, *Movers and Shapers* (Old Tappan, N.J.: Fleming H. Revell, 1988), pp. 15-31.

[3] Ann Spangler and Charles Turner, eds., *Heroes* (Ann Arbor, Mich: Servant Publications, 1985), pp. 26, 27.

[4] V. Z. Bright, ed., *The Greatest Lesson I've Ever Learned,* pp. 153-161.

[5] A. W. Johnson, *Created for Commitment,* pp. 68-71.

[6] C. ten Boom, *The Hiding Place,* pp. 184, 185.

[7] E. G. White, *Steps to Christ,* p. 100.

[8] ———, *The Desire of Ages,* p. 330.

6

# For Emotional Needs

Rita Armstrong had lived on an emotional roller coaster for much of her life. She learned to mask her unhappiness, but often felt weepy and discouraged. Neither medication nor counseling seemed to make any difference.

Then one afternoon she spent several hours meditating on God, His power, and His love from Creation to Calvary. She remembered the certainty she had had as a child that Jesus loved her, then thought of heaven and how loved she would feel when in God's presence at last. The words of Scripture came to her: "Jesus Christ the same yesterday, and to day, and for ever" (Heb. 13:8).

*Jesus cannot change!* Rita thought. *He loved me when I was a child, He will love me when I get to heaven, and He loves me now!* Joy and love overwhelmed her. Suddenly she realized she was significant in His eyes—that she mattered to Him! Jumping to her feet, she began to dance around the house singing over and over, "I matter to God! I matter to God!"[1]

Yes, we do matter to God! How we feel matters to Him. "His heart of love is touched by our sorrows and even by our utterances of them. . . . Nothing that in any way concerns our peace is too small for Him to notice. There is no chapter in our experience too dark for Him to read; there is no perplexity too difficult for Him to unravel."[2]

Rita Armstrong's experience verifies that our feelings matter to God and that contact with Him through the Bible transforms our emotions. The stories in this chapter are of women who found God's Word meeting their emotional needs.

## FROM FEAR TO COURAGE: PSALM 56:3

"What time I am afraid, I will trust in thee."

Barbara Mittleider had reason to fear. It was a pitch-black night, and she had to drive alone to the airport to pick up her husband and a Pastor Ndhlovu. Just a few days earlier one of the secretaries from her office had been murdered. Barbara's route to the airport would go right by the culvert where the police had found the dead woman's body.

Her Volkswagen Beetle did not have room to take their watchdog. With a can of insect repellent as her only weapon she got in the car and began to tremble from fear. She prayed for God's protection, then repeated some words from Psalm 91: "He that dwelleth in the secret place of the most High shall abide under the shadow of the Almighty. I will say of the Lord, He is my refuge and my fortress: my God; in him will I trust" (verses 1, 2).

She later described what happened next. "An immediate sense of calmness and peace came over me as I pulled out into traffic and drove to the airport." The Word had met Barbara's need in a time of fear.[3]

## FROM FRUSTRATION TO PEACE: ISAIAH 26:3

"You will keep in perfect peace him whose mind is steadfast, because he trusts in you" (NIV).

Joni Earickson Tada has had more than her share of frustration. A swimming accident at 17 paralyzed her from the neck down. Life is difficult for Joni because she has to depend totally on others. She has also learned to be totally dependent on God and His Word.

Just a small example. One morning she knocked over a pile of dictation and suddenly felt overcome by her disability. *It's just not fair, Lord,* she thought, waves of self-pity, helplessness, and frustration sweeping over her. *I'm so clumsy! Oh, how I wish I had my hands!*

But just as quickly she pushed away the negative thoughts with words of Scripture. She focused on a verse she had recently memorized: "Put your hope in God, for I will yet praise him, my Savior and my God" (Ps. 42:5, NIV).

Joni still had her problem, but the frustration was gone. A feeling of peace settled in her heart and she was able to go on with her day. "I've trained myself to hold on to some objective anchors from God's Word," she writes.[4]

## FROM STRESS TO CALMNESS: ZEPHANIAH 3:17

"The Lord your God is with you, he is mighty to save. He will take great delight in you, he will quiet you with his love, he will rejoice over you with singing" (NIV).

One morning I awoke to feel the stresses of life at work in my body. My back, head, and feet hurt, and I wasn't even yet out of bed! As I lay there I wondered about the results of my recent mammogram. Why hadn't the doctor called? I thought about all the things that hadn't gotten done the day before. They would have to be added to today's list of chores that was already full. I groaned and rolled over, but finally stumbled out of bed.

"My life is just too full of stress!" I told the Lord as I opened my journal. "What can I do?"

The blank book I was using at the time had a Scripture verse at the bottom of each page. I smiled as I read the ones on the pages that faced me. One was Zephaniah 3:17, and I underlined the phrase "He will quiet you with his love" (NIV).

I imagined myself a little girl coming to my heavenly Father to be held in His arms, hearing Him say, "Now, Dorothy, I'll take care of everything."

The other verse was 1 Peter 5:7: "Cast all your anxiety on him because he cares for you" (NIV). Just what I needed!

I wrote in my journal, "Here, Lord, are some anxieties I can identify this morning. [I listed 14!] Please take them and give me peace; quiet me with Your love. I'm so uptight! I need to relax, to remember that You're in control. Quiet my mind, my heart, and my body."

I could really feel the tension going. Feeling surrounded by my Father's love, I was ready to face my day with calmness. After that encounter with God's Word I was able to breeze through my errands, finishing by midafternoon. I fixed myself some cold lemonade and sat in my garden to enjoy the flowers. It was a good day! What a difference a moment with the Word had made!

"And we know that all things work together for good to them that love God, to them who are the called according to his purpose."

Evelyn Christenson felt under a dark cloud of uncertainty. Her husband, Chris, had cancer. It was Friday, and they had to wait until Monday for tests to discover if the cancer had spread. What did the future hold? She asked the Lord for a promise. She thought of Romans 8:28. It had been her special text since she had miscarried during her first three pregnancies 42 years earlier.

"No, Lord, not *that* old one again!" she cried out in disappointment and frustration.

Evelyn didn't hear an audible voice, but she did sense God speaking a message to her heart. He said, "Evelyn, I want to expand your understanding of this verse. You have thought that you will see Me working all things for your good when you get to heaven and view things from my perspective. But I'm telling you in advance, before Chris even takes the tests next Monday, that I am working for your good whatever the outcome is."

Tears coursed down her cheeks as she felt a wonderful peace and realized she could trust God even before they knew the outcome, that He would work through the circumstances for their good. The tests revealed that the cancer had not spread. Chris had surgery, and his recovery was remarkable.

Three weeks later Evelyn had to undergo a cancer test herself. Once again she focused on God's promise in Romans 8:28. She felt a strong assurance that God was working out His purpose in her life, whatever the outcome would be.

On the morning of her mammogram she remembered the promise in Isaiah 26:3: "Thou wilt keep [her] in perfect peace, whose mind is stayed on thee."

About that morning Evelyn wrote, "Immediately all the tension drained from my body as His peace flooded me. I felt the incredible sense of being completely engulfed in a soft spherical capsule, in the rare atmosphere of God Himself."[5]

## FROM ANGER TO CONTROL: EPHESIANS 4:26

"Be ye angry, and sin not: let not the sun go down upon your wrath."

Anna Stanley is a Christian counselor and frequent speaker at women's seminars. Sometimes she shares how she came to depend on God's Word to deal with anger.

Of phlegmatic temperament, Anna breezed through the first part of her life relaxed, easygoing, and never tempted to be angry. But when menopause hit her, she became a different person. Going from a "quiet, gentle lady" to a "screaming, obnoxious woman," she became impatient and explosive over the smallest incidents. She had a short fuse, and often felt touchy and irritable.

Not knowing where else to go, Anna turned to the Lord and dug deep into Scripture, looking for help to overcome her temper tantrums. One evening, after blowing up at her husband and having to ask his forgiveness, she went to her bedroom and fell on her knees and prayed: "Dear Jesus, I know the Bible is true, I believe every word. Why do I keep blowing up? Teach me how to appropriate Your life as mine. I need that desperately."

Not long after that, while reading Ephesians, she stopped short at verse 26. "Be ye angry, and sin not: let not the sun go down upon your wrath." Anna didn't understand just how to go about doing this, but she decided to let God teach her.

One night as she was driving home with her husband, he said something that hit her the wrong way. Feeling the old anger seething inside, she was about ready to explode. Instead she closed her eyes and prayed silently, *Lord, what Charlie just said makes me very angry. I don't want to sin. Please handle this one for me.*

Quietly the Lord spoke to her heart, *Forgive Charlie.*

Anna reasoned with the Lord. *I don't feel like forgiving him, but I guess I can choose by an act of my will to do it anyway. OK, God, I forgive Charlie.*

Charlie was still driving along talking, unaware of Anna's struggle with her emotions. "As we passed the mailbox at the driveway," she later explained, "a tremendous burden lifted. I had no feelings of anger or resentment."

"I love you, Anna," Charlie said as he switched off the

motor in the garage. He kissed her on the cheek. Tears came to her eyes as she silently thanked the Lord for dealing with her anger.[6]

## FROM DESPAIR TO HOPE: HOSEA 2:15

"I will give her . . . the valley of Achor for a door of hope: and she shall sing there."

Rena Majors grew up in an Adventist home with five sisters, two brothers, and hardworking parents, yet she felt lonely and afraid because of sexual abuse. Eventually pain and despair dogged her path and threatened to overcome her.

Rena admits being angry with God. Why had He let this happen to her? Where was He when she needed Him? He answered her with Isaiah 63:9: "In all their affliction he was afflicted. . . . In his love and in his pity he redeemed them." She knew then that God had been with her in her dark valley. And in that valley she discovered "a door of hope."

Slowly Rena began to heal emotionally. "Without the comfort of the Holy Spirit I would have died in this valley. With each forward motion I am comforted to the degree I allow the truth to cut through the lies. I have been comforted by the promises of God, but first I had to believe them."

Today Rena works with A Door of Hope Ministries, a group of women who share their strength, hope, and experience of healing from sexual abuse and emotional pain. I met Rena in Portland, Tennessee, and was inspired by her joyful buoyancy and her testimony of how God had given her new life and hope.[7]

## SEARCH THE WORD
### Sarah and Hagar
References: Genesis 16; 21:1-20; Hebrews 11:11; *Patriarchs and Prophets*, p. 146.
1. Sarah's Emotions
   a. What feelings do you think Sarah was experiencing during the incidents mentioned in the following verses: Genesis 16:1, 2; 16:3-6; 21:1-7; 21:8, 9; 21:14?
   b. What promises of God's Word did Sarah cling to? (See Gen. 17:15, 16; 17:17-21; 18:11-14.)

c. How did God show that He understood Sarah's emotions? Write down phrases that indicate His sensitivity to her needs.

d. How did God meet Sarah's emotional needs?

2. Hagar's Emotions

a. What feelings do you think Hagar was experiencing during the incidents mentioned in the following verses: Genesis 16:3-5; 16:6-8; 16:9-13; 21:1-8; 21:14-16; 21:17-20?

b. What promises of God's Word did Hagar have to give her courage and hope? (See Gen. 16:10-12; 17:20; 21:13, 18.)

c. Write down the phrases that show that God understood Hagar's emotions and was willing to help her.

d. What did the Lord do to meet Hagar's emotional needs?

PERSONAL DISCOVERIES

1. Make a promise file. Buy some 3" x 5" index cards, a set of dividers, and a file box. Label the dividers with the names of specific emotions, negative or positive, such as joy, hope, peace, patience, trust, anxiety, disappointment, grief, fear, anger, self-control, shame, despair, depression, etc. Read through Psalms and Proverbs looking for promises that apply to these emotions. Copy the promises and file according to the emotion. (Alternate idea: make a promise notebook.)

2. Choose one positive emotion that you need in your life right now. Using a concordance, do a word study on that emotion from Genesis to Revelation. Meditate on one of the verses each day, reading it in several versions, then making your own paraphrase to fit your situation.

3. What kind of God will best meet your emotional needs right now? Read the following metaphors that illustrate one aspect of God's character: Psalm 23; 44:4-8; 46; 91:4; Zephaniah 3:17; Psalm 27:1; 103:13; 18:2; 51:7; 8; Revelation 3:20; Malachi 3:3; Jeremiah 18:6. How does it describe God? What emotional needs does that picture of God fill for you?

GROUP DISCOVERIES

1. Write the names of Bible women on slips of paper and put

them in a bowl. Divide into groups of three or four. Let each group select the names of two or three women from the bowl. Give them five minutes to list the emotional needs of their women, thinking of specific incidents in their lives. How did God meet those needs? Call the groups back together and give each group time to report.

2. Share a time in your life when you depended on the Word to meet an emotional need. Allow others who are willing to share an experience from their own lives of the power of the Word to transform negative emotions into positive ones.

3. Ask the group to list Bible promises. As each promise is given, discuss what emotional need it meets. Or work from the opposite direction: name an emotion and Bible promises that would be meaningful to deal with it. You might want to assign different emotions to each group. Allow about five minutes for group work and another five minutes for feedback.

[1] I. Howat, ed., *Light in the Middle of the Tunnel,* pp. 109-121.

[2] E. G. White, *Steps to Christ,* p. 100.

[3] Rose Otis, ed., *The Listening Heart* (Hagerstown, Md.: Review and Herald Publishing Assn., 1994), pp. 244, 245.

[4] Dale Hanson Bourke, "Joni at 40," *Today's Christian Woman,* January/February 1990.

[5] V. Z. Bright, ed., *The Greatest Lesson I've Ever Learned,* pp. 44-49.

[6] *Ibid.,* pp. 162-168.

[7] Rena Majors, "A Door of Hope," *Southern Tidings,* July 1995.

7

# For Answers
# to Tough Questions

"Flee to the mountains," God impressed Gladys Aylward, so
she left Yangcheng, China, with a hundred orphans between the
ages of 4 and 15. They had no money. It was the middle of the
Sino-Japanese War, and the Japanese had offered a $100 reward
for her capture.

For about two weeks they had wandered through unfamiliar
mountain passes, foraging for food, often sleeping under the stars.
They needed to cross the Yellow River on their journey to safety, but
the Nationalist Army had closed the river to all traffic.

Gladys grappled with some tough questions at the riverbank:
*Where are You, God? Are You still in control? Do You care?* By the
morning of the fourth day she was in despair.

"Remember the story about Moses and the Israelites crossing
the Red Sea?" a teenage girl asked her. "There was no way out for
them, either, but God made a way, didn't He?"

"But I'm not Moses," Gladys sighed.

"But God is still God," the girl replied simply. And of course
He was. He did send a boat for Gladys and her hundred orphans.[1]
Alan Burgess wrote of her experience in *The Small Woman*, and it
was portrayed in a major motion picture, *Inn of the Sixth Happiness.*

This chapter is about those times of darkness and despair,
when we come face-to-face with the tough questions of life. What
do we do when trapped in unbearable circumstances? What do we

do despite death, broken dreams, unrelenting pain, and suffering from which there seems no hope of escape?

Can we depend on the Word in the toughest spots of life? The women in this chapter say "Yes! Even at the worst times you can depend on God. You can depend on His Word to answer life's tough questions: Where is God now? Is He still in control? Does He care?

## WHERE IS GOD NOW?

Jane Grayshon writes of grappling with this question in her book *A Pathway Through Pain.* After years of living with chronic pain and finding no relief through either medicine or prayer, she was disappointed with God. Where was He?

She cried out to Him: "Lord, I feel so confused and unsettled. I yearn to be comforted. . . . Let me see Your eyes, for I know they are full of compassion. Let me feel the tenderness of Your love, which I know is there."

But God was silent. "It was as if He were not there," she says. "As if He had withdrawn. Physically, emotionally, and even spiritually, I felt utterly forsaken."

Through her tears she reached for her Bible and read Psalm 10 and Psalm 13, which expressed her own questions so well: Why are You so far away, O Lord? Why do You hide Yourself when we are in trouble? How much longer will You forget me, Lord? Somehow those words helped her to understand that God was there, even though she couldn't sense His presence just then.

Jane found a God who shared in her suffering more deeply than even her friends or family. Summing up her experience, she writes, "His light shines in our darkness as well as in our day. The place from which we want to escape may be the very place where He is waiting to be found. When we have lost sight of Him altogether we fear Him to have withdrawn; in fact, He has embedded Himself in the darkness within us where we fear even to look." [2]

In her book *Unworld People* Joyce Landorf Heatherley tells of a dark period after her divorce when she felt forsaken by everyone, including God. Numb with pain and unable to concentrate on Bible study or prayer, she cried all the time and seemed unable to do the simplest chores.

One morning while dusting an end table she picked up her

Bible, and it slipped through her fingers to the floor. There it fell open to Romans 8. Her eyes rested on the verses at the close of the chapter. "For I am persuaded, that neither death, nor life, nor angels, nor principalities, nor powers, nor things present, nor things to come, nor height, nor depth, nor any other creature, shall be able to separate us from the love of God, which is in Christ Jesus our Lord" (verses 38, 39).

Joyce carried the Bible to the piano and placed it open on the music rack. Every day after that she spent some time sitting on the piano bench reading those words over and over through her tears, her hurt, and her anger. "I read it when none of the words made sense. I read it when I doubted, and when I couldn't comprehend how God would somehow still love me. I know I was kept alive by God's truth in that passage of Scripture."

Learning of her experience, a cousin personalized one of the verses and embroidered it into a picture that Joyce hung by her bathroom mirror. It said: "Nothing can separate you, Joyce, from the love of God which is in Christ Jesus the Lord."[3]

## IS HE STILL IN CONTROL?

Dorothy Galde asked the question during her college years when she heard that friends of hers, John and Betty Stam, had been murdered in Manchuria by marauding soldiers. They had only begun their ministry. How could such inhumanity exist if God was still in control?

"Read Romans 8:28," advised her father. "Things are always on schedule with God."

Then her young husband died soon after he had begun to practice medicine. They had just moved into their new home, and had eaten only one meal on their new dining room table.

"Any idea that God was in charge fled from me," Dorothy admits. "Things were not on schedule with God. I recoiled at the thought that a just and righteous and loving God could allow this to happen."

Later she remarried and had two children. While her husband was flying planes in Europe during World War II, she had a severe polio attack that left her crippled for life. The disease separated her from her babies for nearly two years.

It seemed more than she could bear. Was God still in control? How could He let such terrible things happen to her if He was?

While meditating on Romans 8:28, she found the answer to her tough questions in the last phrase: "To them who are the called according to his purpose."

Could it be that God's purposes for her hadn't been upset at all by her misfortunes? If He truly was in control, then could His purposes ever be upset? Wouldn't His plans always be on schedule? She thrilled at the realization that in spite of all the tragedies of her life, none of them could derail God's plans for her life, for He was still in control.

After living with her disability for many years, after a fire that destroyed her house and possessions, and after being covered with third-degree burns from that fire, she still insists, "When we let God write the plan for our lives, His purposes are fulfilled. His blueprint is engaged. He is glorified, and so are we."[4]

Katie F. Wiebe, writing in *Alone: A Widow's Search for Joy,* came to a similar conclusion. "He can use even your painful circumstances to glorify Himself. What has happened, has happened. You don't know why. You can't change the situation, but with faith you can accept it, knowing that a sovereign and loving God permitted it. Such acceptance brings the assurance that He is still in control."[5]

## DOES HE CARE?

Darlene D. Rose was a missionary in New Guinea when World War II broke out. Japanese soldiers captured her and her husband and kept them in separate prisoner-of-war camps in the jungle. Just before she was miraculously delivered, she learned that her husband had died.

That night when the lights in the camp were out, she lay face-down on her mat, longing for a soft shoulder to lay her aching head on and someone to put a comforting arm around her. *Lord, are You there?* her breaking heart cried out in the silence of the tropical night. *Do You see my pain? Do You care?*

Just then the Lord spoke quietly to her heart the words of Isaiah 61:1-3: "He hath sent me to bind up the brokenhearted, . . . to comfort all that mourn, . . . to give unto them beauty for ashes, the oil of joy for mourning, the garment of praise for the spirit of heaviness."

So real did His presence seem that she quietly poured out her sorrows to His listening ear, sensing that He took note of every word that she whispered. She knew He understood her oppressive sense of aloneness, the grief too deep for words. Darlene sensed that He wept with her, that He cared.

About that night she later wrote, "I was learning to understand the comfort of the Holy Spirit. Sometime during the dark hours I slept. The sword of sorrow had pierced deep within me, but He had bathed the sword in oil."[6]

Jane Grayshon had a similar encounter with the Word that answered the question Does God care? It was a Monday evening just before Easter in 1980. She was in the hospital critically ill. Her husband, Matthew, and a dozen of their friends had gathered to pray for her.

First they had a session of silent prayer, each person lifting Jane to God in his or her own mind. God seemed especially close to them in the stillness that night.

After the prayer John said, "While I was praying the Lord reminded me of the verse that says 'The steadfast love of the Lord never ceases; his mercies never come to an end.'"

"That's in Lamentations 3," Peter spoke excitedly. "It's amazing because I was thinking of the words of a song that comes from Lamentations 3." He struck a chord on his guitar and sang of God's faithfulness, His steadfast love, and His mercies that never fail.

Matthew was radiant when he visited Jane in the hospital after the prayer meeting. He couldn't wait to open his Bible to Lamentations 3 and share verses 21-32 with her. After that encounter with the Word they felt encouraged that God does indeed care.

Many years later, after years and years of chronic pain, Jane wrote about that evening: "Even though I was not there myself, that special evening in 1980 gave me a profound trust in God's steadfast love—no matter what. Lamentations 3 is a special source of comfort."[7]

PATIENCE IN THE TOUGH TIMES

As Jane Grayshon continued to read the Bible, looking for God's promises, she found herself sometimes growing impatient with God's timetable. She wanted healing now. It was hard to wait through long, dark, painful years and still hang on to His promises. So she asked God for the gift of patience.

Then God impressed her that patience wasn't a gift, but rather a fruit of the Holy Spirit working in her life. So she began praying for the fruit of patience.

"I felt quite subdued as I realized what my prayer actually meant. Patience grows from endurance; endurance from suffering. To pray for patience was very different from praying for the pain to end. It meant opening myself to God, whether or not the pain continued."[8]

It's hard to be patient when the tough times seem never to let up, when suffering and heartache seem never to end. And it's hard to be patient when we claim the promises of God's Word and don't see the answer immediately, or when the answer is not what we expected. Yet we are to keep on depending on the Word.

"When our prayers seem not to be answered, we are to cling to the promise; for the time of answering will surely come, and we shall receive the blessing we need most. But to claim that prayer will always be answered in the very way and for the particular thing that we desire is presumption. God is too wise to err, and too good to withhold any good thing from them that walk uprightly. Then do not fear to trust Him, even though you do not see the immediate answer to your prayers. Rely upon His sure promise, 'Ask and it shall be given you.'"[9]

SEARCH THE WORD
### Woman With the Issue of Blood
References: Matthew 9:20-22; Mark 5:25-34; Luke 8:43-48; *The Desire of Ages,* pp. 342-348.

Historical Note: Later legend names Bernice of Veronica. Eusebius of Caesarea (A.D. 264-340), in his *Ecclesiastical History,* tells of a bronze statue erected to her in Caesarea Philippi.

1. How did this woman's problem affect her life for 12 years? (See Lev. 15:25-33; Mark 5:25, 26; Luke 8:43.) Make a list of all that these texts imply.

2. What risks did she take in seeking out Jesus?

3. What difficulties did she have in locating Jesus? (See *The Desire of Ages,* p. 343.)

4. What caused her persistence in reaching Jesus? (See *The Desire of Ages*, p. 343.)

5. What emotions did the woman experience during the 12 years? during her search for Jesus? when she was healed? when Christ called attention to her healing?

6. What answer did the woman receive to the three tough questions in this chapter? How were these questions answered in her brief contact with the Living Word? Give references to support your statements.

    a. Where is God now?

    b. Is He still in control?

    c. Does He care?

## PERSONAL DISCOVERIES

1. Do a character study on Naomi from the book of Ruth. Notice how she suggested a name change for herself. What did Naomi mean? What did Mara mean? What difficult experiences in life caused her bitterness? Note each incident that mentions Naomi. What emotions did she have? What personality traits did she show? How would she answer the three tough questions from this chapter?

2. Use one of the five methods from chapter 3 to do a detailed chapter study of Romans 8.

3. After reading Romans 8:35-39 in several versions, write your own paraphrase. Personalize it so that it fits your own circumstances. Name the things that threaten to separate you from Christ. Make this passage your personal possession.

## GROUP DISCOVERIES

1. Try to find a different version of the Bible for each member of your group. Read Romans 8:28 and 35-39 aloud, one verse at a time, each person reading from a different version. Discuss your reactions to the various versions.

2. What Bible women faced difficult life situations? Make a list of Bible women who suffered through tough problems. How would they have answered the three tough questions from this chapter?

3. Tell of a time in your life when you asked one or more of the tough questions from this chapter. Explain how you learned to depend on God and His Word. Invite others to share their experiences.

[1] Alan Burgess, *The Small Woman* (New York: E. P. Dutton, 1957), pp. 180-229.

[2] Jane Grayshon, *A Pathway Through Pain* (London: Hodder and Stoughton, 1995), pp. 127-129.

[3] Joyce Landorf Heatherley, *Unworld People* (Austin, Tex.: Balcony Publishing, 1987), pp. 216-222.

[4] Dorothy A. Galde, *You Write the Ticket, Lord* (San Bernardino, Calif.: Here's Life Publishers, Inc., 1983), pp. 17-23, 37-51, 77-91, 111-126, 146.

[5] Katie F. Wiebe, *Alone: A Widow's Search for Joy* (Wheaton, Ill.: Tyndale House Publishers, Inc., 1976), p. 179.

[6] Darlene D. Rose, *Evidence Not Seen* (San Francisco: HarperCollins, 1990), pp. 109-113.

[7] Grayshon, pp. 145-147, 165.

[8] *Ibid.*, pp. 147-149.

[9] E. G. White, *Steps to Christ,* p. 96.

*8*

# For Light
# in the Darkness

As I awoke after midnight in a motel room I tried to remember where the bathroom was. My eyes struggled to focus in the darkness. Shuffling along the side of the bed, I stumbled over my shoes, regained my balance, and reached the end of the bed. Turning left, I groped for the wall. Ouch! I'd forgotten about that chair!

Reaching the wall, I fumbled for a light switch. I tried the other side. Nothing there, either. Nothing on the wall inside. A string brushed my face. Reaching up, I pulled. The light came on. How wonderful to have light!

Life is like that sometimes. The difficulties we face are like a journey into darkness.

### THE WORD BRINGS LIGHT

"When I sit in darkness, the Lord shall be a light unto me," declares the prophet Micah (Micah 7:8). "The Lord is my light," David sang. Christ, the Living Word, is able to light up our darkness, for He is "the light of the world" (John 8:12).

"The entrance of thy words giveth light" (Ps. 119:130). "Thy word is a lamp unto my feet, and a light unto my path" (verse 105). The Living Word and the Written Word are two sources of light for our dark nights.

In her book *You Write the Ticket, Lord,* Dorothy Galde suggests a Four-Point Plan for Disaster that has helped her find the light of God's presence in pain.[1] My summary of her plan is: trust Him, give Him, thank Him, let Him.

## TRUST HIM: ROMANS 8:28

"And we know that all things work together for good to them that love God, to them who are the called according to his purpose."

"When I *know* that whatever catastrophe presently engulfing me has been worked by God into His plan for my life—for eternal good—I can rest," Dorothy Galde states as she looks back on more than her fair share of disasters.

"We have no control of our circumstances," she goes on, but "we make our own mental and spiritual environment. We must believe Him and trust Him; there is no other option for His children."[2]

Barbara Johnson, author of *Stick a Geranium in Your Hat and Be Happy,* would agree. She's had enough dark times to fill several books. In 1966 her husband was in a car accident that left him blind and crippled for months. In 1968 her 18-year-old son died in Vietnam. In 1973 a drunk driver killed a second son. And in 1975 her remaining son told her he was homosexual.

The accumulated pain catapulted Barbara into a dark tunnel of despair. She got in her car and headed for Disneyland, planing to have a fatal crash on the way. The darkness was too much! The pain was too great! But on the way Barbara found the light in her tunnel. She decided to trust the Lord with her son.

"Whatever, Lord. I can't find him. I can't fix him. They tell me he may never come home again. But like Job I am saying Whatever, Lord. Though You slay me, I will trust You."

Her son would return home and back to the Lord many years later, but Barbara didn't know that then. She just made a choice to trust God—to allow His light into her darkness.[3]

"Faith is really faith when things don't work out," James Cress declared in a sermon at the British Columbia camp meeting. "Faith is believing when I don't see it. Faith is trusting if I don't get it."[4] Barbara Johnson had that kind of faith. It's the kind of faith that brings light into our tunnels.

## GIVE HIM: 1 PETER 5:7

"Let Him have all your worries and cares, for he is always thinking about you and watching everything that concerns you" (TLB).

God is waiting for our invitation to carry the burdens for us, to lighten our load. We can choose to give Him our guilt, anger, disappointment, suffering, and grief. When we are able to hand over our pain to God, we are doing something to turn on the light in our tunnel of despair.

"Cast thy burden upon the Lord, and he shall sustain thee" (Ps. 55:22). David had a few catastrophes in his life, but he knew how to find the light in his darkness.

Audrey Wetherell Johnson faced a time of depression while she was a missionary in China. Discovering that the Psalms expressed her emotions of despair better than she could, she began searching them for words that echoed her feelings.

One depressing day she read Psalm 142 and saw a glimmer of light in her darkness. Reading Psalm 143, she used David's words to throw all her worries at the feet of Jesus. Then she came to Psalm 144:1, and the Lord filled her tunnel with a burst of heavenly light. She reread the words "Blessed be the Lord my strength, which teacheth my hands to war, and my fingers to fight."

"Suddenly I was lifted clean out of my depression, knowing that God was my strength and would teach me what to do and think in my present circumstances."[5]

Not long ago I went through a time of darkness. I couldn't bear the pain of the present, but could see no hope for the future. On the outside I was smiling. Inside I was feeling so fragile, splitting apart at my very soul. I couldn't go on in the darkness.

It was then that I read Isaiah 9:2, 3: "The people who walked in darkness have seen a great light. They lived in a land of shadows, but now light is shining on them. You have given them great joy, Lord; you have made them happy" (TEV).

It was but a flicker, but I reached toward it. "Lord, come to me with the light and joy of Your presence," I wrote in my journal. "Lead me out of darkness into Your brightness."

"Bring your shadows to Me," He whispered.

"The shadows in my life are many, Lord," I began. For several minutes I wrote down my concerns for sins, failures, health problems, children, grandchildren, speaking appointments, and writing projects. I handed over nine burdens to the Lord that morning.

In my journal I wrote: "Lord, You are my Light, my Joy, and my Song! Come to me, Lord! Warm my heart; lighten my spirit. Please, Lord, I need You! Oh, how I need You!"

The sun felt as if it were shining for the first time in weeks! Infused with energy and hope, I felt able to face my day with joy. Reading through my journals now, I can see the entries getting more positive, joyful, and hopeful all the time. I have the proof that giving God my burdens really helps.

### THANK HIM: 1 THESSALONIANS 5:18

"In everything give thanks: for this is the will of God in Christ Jesus concerning you."

It was a cold, gray January day. Katie Wiebe sat in the small room that served as her living room, dining room, and kitchen. The three children were still asleep. She needed this quiet time to think through the events of the past few months. It had been a difficult time. Their apartment was too small, and everyone had been sick.

Her husband was 1,500 miles away, where he had collapsed on the way to a church conference. She needed to be with him, but had no idea what to do with the children. The more she thought about her situation, the more discouraged she became.

A quiet voice spoke to her heart: "This is the will of God concerning you." She strained her mind to remember the rest of the verse. She picked up her Bible and began leafing through the New Testament. At last she found it in 1 Thessalonians 5:18: "In every thing give thanks: for this is the will of God concerning you."

*Give thanks for what?* Katie thought. *Give thanks for a sick husband, no money, poor living conditions, sloppy weather, and fussy kids recovering from colds? Lord, there's no way I can see anything in the chaos of my life for which to be thankful!*

Her husband eventually came home but had to have surgery. Her tunnel got darker and longer. *Lord, You know I can't give thanks now!* she complained. *I have too much frustration just trying to be with Walter in the hospital. There's the daily struggle of finding babysitters, missed buses, and trying to be cheerful when there's no money to pay the bills.*

But the verse kept coming back to Katie, and she cautiously began to thank the Lord for each tiny blessing—a volunteer babysitter, encouraging words from doctors, the strength to somehow go on doing what had to be done. Little by little the light came.

"This was my kindergarten lesson," Katie later said. When she had to face being a single parent, she knew where to find the light in Scripture and how to offer the sacrifice of praise.[6]

Dorothy Galde had difficulties with point 3—giving thanks. At the time she wrote her book she had spent 39 years with a disability caused by polio. She could never take a step without checking the floors to make sure there was nothing there to upset her balance. In 39 years she had more than 500 falls, leaving her often bruised and bleeding and weary of the struggle.

"I had to adopt a philosophy that would glorify the Lord. What came about was total thankfulness. I could not fall if I were not walking. Every time I went down, I said, 'Thank You, Lord!' And I meant it."[7]

### LET HIM: 2 CHRONICLES 20:17

"Ye shall not need to fight in this battle: set yourselves, stand ye still, and see the salvation of the Lord."

Let God fight your battles for you. Our darkness is because of Satan. When we suffer it is because we find ourselves caught in the cross fire between good and evil.

"For our struggle is not against flesh and blood," Paul tells us, "but . . . against the powers of this dark world and against the spiritual forces of evil in the heavenly realms" (Eph. 6:12, NIV).

We are never a match for the enemy, and even less so when we are weary from pain and heartache, grief and depression. Ellen White advises: "Often your mind may be clouded because of pain. Then do not try to think. You know that Jesus loves you. He understands your weakness. You may do His will by simply resting in His arms."[8]

"Satan is well aware that the weakest soul who abides in Christ is more than a match for the hosts of darkness."[9] No wonder he seeks to discourage us. He delights to see us groping, and wants us to stumble. The devil doesn't want us to find the light. So he does all he can to keep us from Christ and His Word.

In her book *Soaring on Broken Wings* Kathy Bartalsky relates her journey through tragedy, heartache, and bitter loss. Two of her children died. While serving as a missionary in Africa, she had debilitating bouts of malaria that left her weary and depressed. Then her husband, a mission pilot, died in a plane crash. Her world caved in, and all was black.

Then Kathy reached for the light. Immersing herself in God's Word, she found her peace in His promises, her light in His presence. She was willing to let Him fight the battles for her.

Looking back on her experiences, she writes, "Death, illness, heartache, tragedy, loneliness, sin, greed, persecution, danger—none of these earthly things is the battleground. The battleground is the soul. Without Christ we battle alone—and lose. With Christ . . . we are more than conquerors."[10]

SEARCH THE WORD
### Hannah's Light
References: 1 Samuel 1, 2; *Patriarchs and Prophets,* pp. 569-580.

1. Do a study in contrasts with Hannah (meaning "grace") and Peninnah (meaning "red pearl"). Draw a line down the middle of a sheet of paper. List Hannah's characteristics on one side with Peninnah's on the other. Study the following areas: personality/temperament, religious commitment, total children, talents/abilities, emotions.

2. What laws governed Jewish polygamous marriages? (Deut. 21:15-17)

3. Measure Hannah's handling of her life's difficulties according to this chapter's Four-Point Plan for Disaster. Copy statements that show how she participated in each of these areas.

　　a. Trust Him. (Trust Him to keep His promises.)
　　b. Give Him. (Give Him your burdens and griefs.)
　　c. Thank Him. (Praise Him in all circumstances.)
　　d. Let Him. (Let Him fight your battles.)

4. What advice would Hannah have for the dark times of your life? What makes you think she might understand?

PERSONAL DISCOVERIES
1. Read 1 Samuel 1:3, 11. Notice the phrase "Lord of hosts." This is the first time Scripture uses that title for God. The Hebrew words are Yahweh seba'oth. It means He is the commander of all

created beings, the one who will lead His creation to final victory. "The title 'Lord of hosts' is perhaps the most sublime of God's titles. It is suggestive of His full control and overlordship of the entire universe."[11] Look up these references where this title for God appears: Psalm 24:9, 10; Psalm 46:7; Psalm 84:1, 3, 8, 12.

2. Hannah also had a good knowledge of the Scripture available at that time—the books of Moses and Job. Look up the cross-references for the following verses from 1 Samuel 2: verse 2 (Ex. 15:11; Deut. 4:35); verse 6 (Job 5:18); verse 7 (Job 1:21); verse 8 (Job 36:7; 38:4-6).

3. Eleven references to psalms are given for Hannah's song. It is possible that some of these were already in existence in her day and familiar to her. Scholars suspect that many of the psalms came from her time or before.[12] The psalms cross-referenced are Psalms 2, 9, 18, 37, 75, 89, 91, 92, 94, 96, and 113. You may want to compare them with Hannah's song to look for similarities of expression.

4. Write a prayer based on the Four-Point Plan outlined in this chapter—Trust Him, Give Him, Thank Him, and Let Him—using one verse or paragraph for each point. Let it tell of your personal experience with the Lord in the midst of trouble.

5. Do a word study on the word *light*. Make three lists: God as the light; the Word as the light; and us as the light.

GROUP DISCOVERIES

1. Which of the four points covered in this chapter do you feel is the hardest to do: trust Him when you don't understand; give Him all your burdens; thank Him for everything; let Him fight your battles? Why?

2. Share a time something you thought was a tragedy in your life really turned out to be a blessing in disguise.

3. Discuss the following questions. How do you think Hannah's marriage with its joys and griefs compares to situations of divorce and remarriage today? Do you think Hannah should have petitioned God for a child, or should she have been satisfied with the love of her husband? How is it possible that women with children might make life more difficult for those who are barren?

4. When you are going through a tough time in life, groping your way in the darkness, how would you like people to show sen-

sitivity to your problem? What are some things you wish they would *not* say? Share experiences, positive or negative.

[1] D. A. Galde, *You Write the Ticket, Lord,* pp. 139-146.

[2] *Ibid.*, pp. 143, 146.

[3] Barbara Johnson, *Stick a Geranium in Your Hat and Be Happy* (Dallas: Word Publishing, 1990), pp. 35-48: Nancie Carmichael, "A Funny Woman Gets Serious," *Virtue,* March/April 1995.

[4] Jim Cress, camp-meeting sermon, British Columbia, July 1995.

[5] A. W. Johnson, *Created for Commitment,* pp. 348, 349.

[6] K. F. Wiebe, *Alone,* pp. 16-29.

[7] Galde, pp. 141, 142.

[8] E. G. White, *The Ministry of Healing,* p. 251.

[9] ———, *The Great Controversy* (Mountain View, Calif.: Pacific Press Publishing Assn., 1911), p. 530.

[10] K. Bartalsky, *Soaring on Broken Wings,* pp. 181-192.

[11] *The Seventh-day Adventist Bible Commentary* (Hagerstown, Md.: Review and Herald Publishing Assn., 1953), vol. 1, p. 173.

[12] *Ibid.*, vol. 3, pp. 618, 619.

*9*

# The Basis for Doing

Audrey locked herself in her bedroom, determined to discover what she believed. Not bothering to turn on a light, she went to her window, opened it, and called out to the starlit sky, "God, if there be a God, if You will give me some philosophy that makes reasonable sense to me, I will commit myself to follow it."

She had grown up in a Christian home, then gave up her belief in Jesus Christ and the Bible under the influence of her university professors. However, to become an atheist seemed just as unreasonable to her.

*I guess I'm an agnostic,* she decided. *I don't know for sure there is a God, but then again, I'm not sure there isn't.*

Pacing the floor, she pondered the different philosophies she had studied. But she couldn't concentrate. She heard a small voice inside her head repeating "Believest thou that I am the Son of God?"

*No, of course not! I've already settled that question,* she thought. *The Bible doesn't make sense to me. Those miracle stories—Jonah and the whale, Noah and the Flood, and the virgin birth—can't be true!* But the question wouldn't leave her. "Believest thou that I am the Son of God?"

Sitting on her bed, Audrey began to think about the mystery of life itself. *I don't understand that either,* she pondered. *But I am alive!* Her mind reached out to God to grasp His reality. And then God came to her.

"Suddenly God's mysterious revelation was given to me. I

could not reason out the mystery of the Incarnation, but God caused me to know that this was a fact. I knelt down in tears of joy and worshiped Him as Saviour and Lord." And Audrey knew that if she accepted the reality of Jesus Christ in her life she must believe His Word, even though it didn't seem reasonable to believe.

She began a diligent search of the Bible, reasoning, *If Jesus Christ is the Son of God, then He will not lie.* Studying the gospel, she found that He spoke of the miracles in the Old Testament as fact.

Audrey came to understand that she must take by faith that the Bible was God's Word and the complete and only authority for her life.[1] In doing so, Audrey Wetherell Johnson had discovered the basis for doing. It is expressed simply in Mary's statement to the servants at the wedding in Cana: "Whatsoever he saith unto you, do it" (John 2:5).

If you and I are to be doers of the Word, then, like Mary and Audrey, we must come to the place where we accept the absolute authority of God's Word. There can be no question in our minds. The Bible is God's truth, His will, His divine message and direction for our lives. Unless we believe this, we will never step out to do it.

Using the letters of the word b-a-s-i-s as an acrostic, we will examine what it means to make God's Word our basis for doing.

## B—BELIEVE THAT THE BIBLE IS GOD'S INSPIRED WORD

Dr. Helen Huston, who spent her life as a missionary physician in Nepal, had her struggles with this principle soon after her graduation from medical college.

"The Bible was a major hang-up for me," she admits. In medical school a professor had mocked the Genesis story of Creation as unacceptable to science. Helen figured that God gave her a brain and He expected her to use it. By her reasoning, much of the Bible could not be true. And those doubts kept her from having a personal relationship with Jesus Christ.

In spite of her doubts, Helen went as a missionary to India. While taking language study, she realized she didn't have the vibrant faith that others possessed. She longed for it, but didn't know how to get it. Then she talked to Jay, a fellow student.

"I'm wrestling spiritually," Helen admitted. "I feel empty and hollow inside. I don't understand the Bible. The cross is a mystery."

Jay gave her a booklet that led her to search the Scriptures. There she came face-to-face with one of Christ's commands: "You shall love the Lord your God with all your heart and with all your soul and with all your mind."[2] Helen struggled with faith and doubt. Faith won out, and she made a complete surrender to Jesus Christ and His Word. It changed her life.

About the problem of doubt, Ellen White says: "God never asks us to believe, without giving sufficient evidence upon which to base our faith. His existence, His character, the truthfulness of His word, are all established by testimony that appeals to our reason; and this testimony is abundant. Yet God has never removed the possibility of doubt. Our faith must rest upon the evidence, not demonstration."[3]

## A—ACCEPT THE AUTHORITY OF GOD'S WORD IN YOUR LIFE

Catherine Marshall stood at a crossroad. Some friends pointed in one direction, and others urged the opposite way. She was confused until she decided to trust the Word.

"I decided to go to the one place I could count on for final authoritative truth—the Bible," she writes. "Scripture had never yet led me astray. From long experience I knew that . . . the Bible still is 'the only infallible rule of faith and practice.'"[4]

I had a similar struggle when I was 14 years old and attending public school. When a friend invited me to a party at a skating rink on Friday night, I wanted to go, but it conflicted with what my parents had taught me about Sabbath observance.

"We won't do anything bad," my friend urged. "Please come. Everyone is coming!" Uncertain what to say, I answered that I'd have to ask my mother.

"Dorothy, you know what the Bible says," my mother said. "You know what I believe. You know what you want to do. I will not decide for you. This is a decision between you and God."

Wisely Mother threw the ball in my court! I struggled all night with my problem and found peace only when I accepted God's Word as the authority in my life.

I prayed that night, "OK, God. You say to 'remember the Sabbath day.' That's Your Word, and I will follow it." That decision was probably the most important one of my teenage years.

Having God's Word as my authority has solved many problems for me during the past 40-plus years.

## S—SURRENDER YOURSELF TO OBEY THE WORD

Recently I read of the wonderful accomplishments of Jeanie Gilchrist, a single missionary in Africa. I discovered the basis for all of her accomplishments in one statement by her biographer.

"The Word of God was her guidebook; in it she found her path. To its commands she bowed, yielding a hearty, unhesitating obedience to all that she knew of the will of God."[5]

Mary Slessor experienced a similar surrender to the Word. "The Bible became her constant companion, and from its pages she gathered stores of wisdom and strength. Instead of questioning, she read the Holy Book, and then she found that it changed her heart and altered her outlook and doings." Surrender to the authority of the Word was her secret of success as a worker for God.[6]

Amy Carmichael is another woman whose life story has inspired me. She did amazing things and accomplished the impossible. I think I see the reason in an entry in her journal.

"My vow: Whatsoever Thou sayest unto me, by Thy grace I will do it. . . . My joy: To do Thy will, O God. . . . My prayer: Conform my will to Thine." She surrendered herself to obey the Word.[7]

## I—IMPLEMENT THE WORD IN YOUR LIFE

This is the crux of the matter—allowing the Word to influence your actions, to change the things you do and how you do them.

Sallie Clingman tells of her struggle to put the Word into practice. She was at a Bible conference when one of the speakers preached on James 1:2-4 and 1 Thessalonians 5:16 and the need to thank God in the midst of trial.

Sallie hurried from the meeting to the privacy of her room. It was stifling hot, so she went out onto the fire escape to cool off and to think. She was experiencing difficulties in her life. The tears flowed freely as she struggled with the Word.

"Lord, how can I consider it a joy to go through all I'm going through? How can I do what Your Word says?"

Finally she concluded that either she accepted the authority of God's Word or she didn't. And if she did, then she must do what

He asked her to do. Sallie whispered a simple prayer: "God, I want to thank You for all the discomfort I have experienced these weeks. Thank You for the loneliness, thank You for the lousy self-image. You know what You are doing. I trust You."

Her mood changed. She forgot about her trials as she began to praise God. Sallie now testifies, "God's Word, when trusted and obeyed, really changed my life."[8]

## S—SET THE WORD UP AS YOUR REFERENCE POINT

Ruth Bell Graham talks about the Word of God being her reference point. In her book *It's My Turn* she tells about what can happen when we do not have a reliable central reference point.

It seems that the Pennsylvania State Highway Department once set out to build a bridge. It had two crews working from opposite banks of the river. When the two segments of the bridge came together in midstream, they were 13 feet out of line. Each crew had worked from its own reference point.

Our reference point as Christian women is the Word of God—the Living Word and the Written Word. The problem with many of us today is that we have lost our reference point.[9]

Author Eileen Guder would agree. She states, "I believe that the first question we must ask about any attitude, plan, project, or proposal is, 'Does this square with what I know of God's will as I read it in the Scripture?' "[10]

In the same vein, Ellen White writes, "Our only safety is found in obedience to God's Word, which has been given us as a sure guide and counselor."[11]

## LOTTIE MOON'S BASIS FOR DOING

Lottie Moon, missionary to China, was in love with a man named Crawford, a professor at Harvard University. Planning a spring wedding, she gave notice to the mission board that she was leaving China. Lottie loved her young man passionately, but she also loved her Lord, and this caused conflict. Crawford did not believe in the inspiration of the Bible. Laughing at the idea that God made the world in six days, he believed that human beings had evolved over millions of years.

*How can I live the rest of my life with someone who believes so differ-*

*ently?* Lottie wondered. *I know he doesn't feel the call to mission service that I do. Will that be a problem in the years to come? Will I end up breaking my covenant with God in order to keep my covenant with Crawford?*

Lottie's mind kept coming back to the Word. Her plans and God's plans as revealed in the Word had come into conflict. She finally decided she must be true to her reference point. The Word must be the basis for her decision, regardless of how much she loved Crawford and longed to spend the rest of her life with him.

Years later someone asked her if she regretted that decision. "God had first claim on my life," she explained, "and since the two conflicted, there could be no question about the result." [12]

SEARCH THE WORD
## The Wedding in Cana
References: John 2:1-12; *The Desire of Ages,* pp. 144-153.

1. **Place**: Cana of Galilee, eight miles north of Nazareth and five miles north and east of Sepphoris. Locate them on a map.

    a. How long did it take Jesus and His disciples to reach Cana? (John 2:1)

    b. Where did they travel from? How far was it? (John 1:28)

2. **Time**: Beginning of Christ's public ministry, late autumn, A.D. 27 (*The Seventh-day Adventist Bible Commentary,* vol. 5, p. 230).

    a. What festival took Jesus, and all male Jews, to Jerusalem in the fall of A.D. 27? (Lev. 23:34)

    b. What three major events happened on that journey? (Matt. 3:4; Luke 3, 4; John 1)

3. **The Wedding Feast**

    a. Why were Mary and Jesus invited?

    b. How long did such feasts last? (Judges 14:12)

    c. Why were the waterpots at the feast? (Mark 7:1-3. *The Seventh-day Adventist Bible Commentary* describes how they did this.)

    d. How much did each waterpot hold? (One firkin equaled seven and one-half gallons.) Estimate the number of guests.

4. **The Characters**: Bride, bridegroom, master of the feast, Mary, Jesus, disciples, servants, guests.

    a. Name the five disciples. (John 1:35-51)

b. When she heard the disciples' testimony, "We have found him, of whom Moses in the law, and the prophets, did write" (John 1:45), what words of the angel and of Anna do you think she remembered? (See Luke 1 and 2.) What Old Testament prophecies must have been on her mind? (See marginal references.)

c. What evidence do you find that Mary placed authority in God's Word?

5. **The Application**

a. With which of the characters of this story do you most identify with at this time in your life?

b. In what area of your life do you need to see the water turned into wine—to see God work a miracle?

c. If you could talk to Mary right now, what impossibilities in your life would you share with her?

d. What advice do you think Mary would share with you?

## PERSONAL DISCOVERIES

1. Make a list of Bible characters to whom God gave a direct command. What were the results of accepting or rejecting the authority of His Word? Try to come up with a list of 10 people. Locate and read their stories.

2. Read the following verses about "doing the Word": Revelation 22:14; James 1:22-25; Hebrews 13:20, 21; Matthew 7:21; Matthew 7:24; John 13:17; Luke 6:46-49. Choose one of them to paraphrase, putting your name into the verse.

3. Choose one book of the Bible. Read through it looking for commands. Underline the commands in green. Try to put one of those commands into practice each day.

## GROUP DISCOVERIES

1. Share a time you had to choose between following people and the Word of God. What has it meant in your life to have the Word of God as your reference point?

2. Give each woman a copy of 1 Peter 3. Read through it together and underline 10 command passages. Divide into groups of two or three. Give each group one command to discuss for five minutes. What do you think this verse meant to the people in

Peter's day? How can we implement this command today? Allow time for feedback.

3. Read together the parable of the wise man and the foolish man in Luke 6:47-49. Read it again as the wise woman and the foolish woman. Divide into groups of four or five. Let each group follow the pattern of this parable, but use a more feminine occupation to illustrate the point. After 10 or 15 minutes, call the groups back together to share their parables.

[1] A. W. Johnson, *Created for Commitment,* pp. 40-43.

[2] Gerald W. Hankins, *A Heart for Nepal* (Winnipeg, Man.: Windflower Communications, 1992), pp. 30-35.

[3] E. G. White, *Steps to Christ,* p. 105.

[4] A. Spangler and C. Turner, eds., *Heroes,* pp. 50, 51.

[5] J. J. Ellis, *Jeanie Gilchrist* (Kilmarnock, Scotland: John Ritchie), pp. 76, 77.

[6] —— *Mary Slessor* (Kilmarnock, Scotland: John Ritchie), p. 12.

[7] Spangler and Turner, pp. 30, 31.

[8] V. Z. Bright, ed., *The Greatest Lesson I Ever Learned,* pp. 50-56.

[9] Elizabeth R. Skoglund, *Wounded Heroes* (Grand Rapids: Baker Book House, 1992), pp. 193, 194.

[10] Joyce Blackburn, *Roads to Reality* (Old Tappan, N.J.: Fleming H. Revell Co., 1979), p. 38.

[11] Ellen G. White, *Counsels on Health* (Mountain View, Calif.: Pacific Press Publishing Assn., 1951), p. 290.

[12] H. I. Smith, *Movers and Shapers,* pp. 90-108; David and Naomi Shibley, *The Smoke of a Thousand Villages* (Nashville: Thomas Nelson Publishers, 1989), pp. 63-67.

# 10

# The Heart
# for Doing

She was only a teenager, but Mary of Nazareth had a heart for
doing God's will. Can you imagine her fear when she understood
the angel's message? The implications must have been scary. Yet
she didn't run away. She opened her heart and listened to Him,
her mind comparing it with promises of the Messiah she had
learned from her study of the Old Testament.

"And Mary said, Behold the handmaid of the Lord; be it unto
me according to thy word" (Luke 1:38). Note the phrase "according
to thy word." Mary believed the angel's message to be God's word.
She didn't understand how, but she trusted His promises and was
submissive to His will. Mary had a heart for doing God's word.

Like Mary, we too can have a heart for doing God's will—one
that is open, willing, submissive, and obedient.

## AN OPEN HEART

Ney Bailey, a new Christian intent on learning God's will, enrolled for a class on the book of Romans. One of the assignments was
to go through Romans and find everything Paul said about faith.

She discovered more than three dozen references to faith. After
some study, she concluded that faith is simply taking God at His
word, believing what He says, and acting upon it. In other words,
faith is "doing the Word."

"I began to see clearly that faith is not a feeling," Ney writes.

"It is a choice we have—to take God at His word. As a result, I made a lifetime commitment to bank my life on God's Word."

It wasn't long before she began to realize that God wanted her relationship with her father to change. Things hadn't gone well with them since her teen years. He had hurt her, and she repaid him with hostility and separation. The rift was wide. And now she sensed that God wanted her to do something about it. "What, Lord? Show me what to do," she prayed as she searched the Word.

God led her to 1 Corinthians 13. She put her name in the chapter, "Ney is patient; Ney is kind; Ney is not provoked," and knew it was not true. Then she remembered that God is love. She read the chapter again, putting God's love into the chapter. Now it read "God's love toward me is kind; God's love toward me is patient; God's love toward me is not provoked."

*Wow!* Ney thought. *I can't believe God loves me like that!* And then a new idea lit her mind. *And God loves my dad in exactly the same way as He loves me! Wow!*

Ney realized her love for her father had been conditional, but that God was asking her to love her dad just as He loved her—unconditionally. She was not to wait for him to change, but she was to alter her attitude and love him anyway, just as he was.

That was hard for Ney. She had to forgive her dad for all the times he had hurt her, not because he had asked her forgiveness, but because God had requested it of her. She went to visit her father, and their relationship was restored. Not long after that he died.

At the funeral Ney looked at her father's casket and thought, *I'm so glad I obeyed God's Word and forgave Dad even when I didn't feel like it. Now I have no regrets except that I wish I had done it sooner!*[1]

Ney Bailey had a heart open to God's will. Her experience reminds me of David's when he prayed, "Teach me to do thy will; for thou art my God" (Ps. 143:10).

## A WILLING HEART

Ellen Harmon did not have a willing heart when the Lord told her, "Make known to others what I have revealed to you."

"Lord, no, please!" she begged on her knees in prayer. "Tell someone else to do it. It's too hard for me. I'm weak and shy and only 17. I can't do it, Lord."

"I want you to do this," He assured her. "My grace is sufficient for you. I will hold you up. Don't be afraid."

She struggled for many days, not wanting to do what God was asking of her. Her friends prayed for her, and eventually she opened her heart to His will. Later she wrote, "I committed myself to the Lord, ready to do His bidding, whatever that might be."[2]

In yielding herself to God without reservation, Ellen reminds me of the Israelites in the wilderness who were noted for bringing "a willing offering" (Ex. 35:29) to the Lord. For the next 70 years Ellen had a heart willing to do God's word.

### A SUBMISSIVE HEART

Catherine also struggled to have a willing heart. Shy by nature, she found it difficult to talk to others about the Lord. She knew she should give her testimony, but shrank from speaking before a crowd. And she knew she should visit her neighbors, but she feared being rejected.

Then one day while passing through a poor neighborhood in London she felt the Lord urging, "Speak to these people about Me, Catherine."

*Am I imagining things?* Catherine wondered. *Or is God really talking to me? If He is, I suppose I must try.* Fearfully she looked around for someone to speak to, then saw a woman dressed in shabby clothes sitting on her doorstep with a jug in her hand.

*I'll bet she's drunk,* Catherine thought. *She doesn't want to be bothered, but I guess I must say something.*

Catherine's knees shook as she approached the woman, forcing a smile. "Would you like to come to chapel with me?" she asked.

"Can't!" the woman replied. "Have to look after my husband. He's drunk inside."

"Let me talk to him," Catherine offered.

"No use tryin'. He's too drunk to understand," his wife hedged. When Catherine insisted, the woman led her inside to where her husband sat bleary-eyed, an empty jug beside his chair.

*Lord, what have You gotten me into?* Catherine silently prayed. *What can I say to such a man?* She opened her Bible to Luke 15 and read the story of the prodigal son. The man stared at her through bloodshot eyes, trying to focus on her words.

"God loves you like that father," Catherine told him. A tear trickled down the man's cheek. That was the beginning of Bible studies with that family. Within a few weeks Catherine had a Bible study class of 11 alcoholics, including this man.

Catherine's heart was opening up. She felt willing to do whatever God asked her to do. One day she told a thousand people in her husband's church, "You may have thought me to be an obedient Christian, but I haven't been at all. God has been asking me to speak for Him, and I have not done it because I was afraid. Now I have promised the Lord that from this moment on, I will be obedient."

For Catherine Mumford Booth, that decision began a lifetime of preaching and service for the poor of London. We know her today as cofounder of the Salvation Army.[3]

Catherine Mumford Booth found joy in obeying the command "Submit yourselves therefore to God" (James 4:7). Hers was a submissive heart.

## An Obedient Heart

Ruth Bell Graham awoke at 3:00 in the morning and thought of a son who was running from God. Fear gripped her heart. She was thousands of miles away from him. What might he be up to now? Her imagination came up with plenty of things he might be doing, and thinking about it only made her feel worse.

Then in the stillness of the night she sensed God speaking to her heart. "Ruth, quit studying the problems and start studying the promises."

Smiling, she turned on the light and reached for her Bible. The verse that came to mind was Philippians 4:6: "Be careful for nothing; but in every thing by prayer and supplication with thanksgiving let your requests be made known unto God." Ruth pondered that awhile. Then she read the next verse. "And the peace of God, which passeth all understanding, shall keep your hearts and minds through Christ Jesus."

*So that's it!* Ruth felt as though the light in her mind had just been switched on. *Thanksgiving is the missing ingredient in my prayers. I'll do it, Lord. I'll start right now!*

Ruth began praising the Lord for His goodness. She thanked Him for His blessings to her husband and their marriage, for her children, for the ways she saw Him working in their lives. Then she thanked Him for the difficult times she'd gone through, and the lessons she had learned. Those early-morning hours became a praise session!

By the time she had finished, Ruth felt wonderful. Her fears were gone. God's peace was in her heart.[4]

Ruth Bell Graham had demonstrated what it means to have an obedient heart. I think Isaiah must have had people like Ruth in mind when he wrote about the blessings God will give to those who are "willing and obedient" (Isa. 1:19).

I feel challenged by such godly women as Ney, Ellen, Catherine, and Ruth, who had hearts willing to do God's will. Open hearts. Submissive hearts. Obedient hearts.

*Lord, help me to have a heart like theirs—open to Your teaching, willing to be led, submissive to Your will, obedient to Your commands.*

SEARCH THE WORD
## Women With Willing Hearts
Many women in Scripture had hearts willing to do God's will. Read the stories below and answer the questions about each woman.

1. Genesis 6-8—Noah's Wife
   a. What indication of God's will did she have?
   b. What feelings do you think she had during this experience?
   c. What obstacles, trials, and difficulties did she face?
   d. What was her reward for having a willing heart?
2. Genesis 24—Rebekah
   a. What indication of God's will did she have?
   b. What feelings do you think she had during this experience?
   c. What obstacles, trials, and difficulties did she face?
   d. What was her reward for having a willing heart?
3. Exodus 1:15-22—Shiphrah and Puah
   a. What indication of God's will did they have?
   b. What feelings do you think they had during this experience?
   c. What obstacles, trials, and difficulties did they face?
   d. What was their reward for having a willing heart?

## PERSONAL DISCOVERIES

1. Do similar studies about the following women who also had willing hearts to do whatever God asked them to do. Sarah (Gen. 12:1-5); Esther (Esther 1-10); Rahab (Joshua 2-6, Heb. 11:31); Deborah (Judges 4; 5); Jochebed (Ex. 2:1-10; Heb. 11:23).

2. Do Ney Bailey's experiment with 1 Corinthians 13. Write out a paraphrase of this definition of love, putting your own name in place of the word *love*. Then do it a second time, putting "God's love toward me" in place of the word *love*.

3. Read Philippians 4:6, 7 in as many versions as you have available. Write your own paraphrase of what it means to you. Then try Ruth Bell Graham's experiment with praise and thanksgiving. Make as long a list as possible of things you are thankful for, even including the difficult situations in your life right now. Praise Him for what He is doing in the midst of your trials and problems.

## GROUP DISCOVERIES

1. Share an experience when you found it difficult to have a willing heart to do what you knew God wanted you to do.

2. Divide into groups of three to five. Assign each group one of the following women with willing hearts: Sarah, Esther, Rahab, Deborah, or Jochebed. Assign the texts as given under "Personal Discoveries," exercise 1. Allow them time to read their stories together and come up with the answers to the four basic questions in Search the Word.

3. Think about a difficult situation you face. Then find something to praise God for in that situation. Let those who are willing share their praise.

---

[1] V. Z. Bright, ed., *The Greatest Lesson I've Ever Learned,* pp. 20-27.

[2] See Ellen G. White, *Life Sketches* (Mountain View, Calif.: Pacific Press Publishing Assn., 1915), pp. 64-73.

[3] Lewann Sotnak, *Their Light Still Shines* (Minneapolis: Augsburg Press, 1993), pp. 60-65; Jenty Fairbank, *William and Catherine Booth: God's Soldiers* (London: Hodder and Stoughton, 1974), p. 45.

[4] Bright, pp. 94-97.

*11*

# The Act
# of Doing

Mildred Cable went to Mongolia because God commanded, "Go ye into all the world, and preach the gospel to every creature" (Mark 16:15). It was dangerous, but Mildred didn't worry, for she was there in obedience to God's Word.

At one point a young rebel, a man known as General Thunderbolt, and his 3,000 men terrorized the countryside. The outlaws rode through the villages plundering, raping, and killing. They captured Mildred Cable and took her to the hideout of their general to treat his wounds. After he was better, she asked permission to leave. They granted it.

As she was preparing to leave she thought, *I wonder if this is the purpose for which God brought me here. I must witness to this wicked man.* Then the words of Ezekiel 33:8 came clearly to mind: "When I say unto the wicked, . . . thou shalt surely die; if thou dost not speak to warn the wicked from his way, . . . his blood will I require at thine hand."

There it was—a direct command from the Lord. It was a call to obedience to the authoritative Word of God. Because she had a heart for doing, Mildred knew that she must act upon that word. Choosing her best Bible, one with gold lettering, she wrapped it in bright-red paper. Taking the present with her, she went to face the Thunderbolt, though she realized her action might cost her life. Nevertheless, in obedience to God's command, she did it.

"Great Man, we have received your hospitality for many weeks," Mildred said diplomatically. "I'm glad I could help you recover. This gift is of great value. It is the Word of the Living God. It is for you."

The general rose to his feet and stared at Mildred with a frown on his hardened face.

"This Book warns men to prepare to meet God," she continued. "I beg you to repent of your evil ways. Please accept this Book. Read it; obey it. Accept the salvation it offers through Jesus Christ." There—she had done it. She stood quietly awaiting the Thunderbolt's reaction. All was silent. Mildred could feel her heart beating rapidly. Would he accept?

The general saluted, took her gift, and bowed. Turning, she walked from the room, her mission accomplished.[1]

The basis for Mildred Cable's courage was in the absolute authority of Scripture. She had a heart willing to do the Word, but more important, she followed through with the acts of obedience.

But an obedient heart is not enough. We must also have obedient feet, hands, eyes, ears, and tongues.

## MARY IS AN EXAMPLE

Mary, the mother of Jesus, is an example of someone who followed through on her commitment to the Word of God. Not only did she believe in the authority of God's Word—not only did she have a submissive heart—but Mary did the acts of obedience, she "performed all things according to the law of the Lord" (Luke 2:39).

It was one thing to say "Yes, Lord, be it unto me even as thou wilt," but quite another to hang in there through nine months of illegitimate pregnancy, to put up with the scorn of her peers. And it was easy enough to say she would bear the Messiah, but quite another to feed Him, change Him, clothe Him, and teach Him.

She and Joseph were careful to do all the acts of obedience required by the laws of Moses as recorded in Scripture, as well as the commands delivered through the angel:

1. They circumcised Jesus on the eighth day.
2. They called His name Jesus.
3. They observed the ritual of purification after 40 days.
4. They offered the required sacrifice of turtledoves.

5. They went to Egypt and returned.

6. They taught Jesus Scripture.

Mary's surrender to the Word of God was complete from the set of her will right through to her actions.

GOD'S WORD IS REASON ENOUGH

Steve Bartalsky was excited about his mission assignment to Africa with Helimission. His wife, Kathy, wasn't so enthusiastic. They had funds to raise, paperwork to complete on the adoption of a child, a house to sell, and their goods to pack. She had qualms at times about leaving the security of a good job in the United States to take up self-supporting mission work.

One afternoon she walked to a nearby irrigation canal to seek God's will. She had her Bible along and stopped from time to time to read a passage that came to mind. At one point she opened to Philippians 3:8, 10, 11. Those verses burned into her heart. It seemed to be God's personal message just for her.

"I consider everything a loss compared to the surpassing greatness of knowing Christ Jesus my Lord. . . . I want to know Christ and the power of his resurrection and the fellowship of sharing in his sufferings" (NIV).

Kathy walked in the warm Phoenix sunshine meditating on those words. It seemed the Lord was saying to her, "Kathy, your need to know Me should surpass any desire you have to serve Me anywhere. Don't focus on your doubts. I'll take care of the problems. Your job is to go. The most important thing is that you simply obey Me. Go because I say so and for no other reason." [2]

God's command has been reason enough for countless women who have felt called to do a work for God. Because they believed God's Word was the final answer, they responded and went.

Elizabeth Fry read the words of Matthew 25 and believed that God was asking her to take His love to the suffering and needy in prisons. She fought government officials and public opinion in order to do what she believed God was telling her to do. Christ's teachings formed her point of reference. [3]

Annie Taylor's obedience took her to the remote kingdom of Tibet. She was the first Christian woman to enter that country. Coworkers told her not to go, that Tibet was closed to Christian missions, that it was too dangerous for a woman to undertake such a journey, that she would fail and might even lose her life.

But Annie Taylor declared, "We have received no orders from the Lord that are impossible to be carried out." If God wanted her in Tibet, then she would go to Tibet. Her biography is a thrilling account of what one woman can accomplish when she trusts God's Word completely and acts upon it.[4]

## FAITH ACTS IN SPITE OF DIFFICULTIES

Gladys Aylward responded to God's call to go. She believed God wanted her in China, so she went for an interview in London. Mission authorities told her, "Find a way to serve God in England. You are too old to learn a new language. Your marks in school are not high enough. You don't have what it takes."

Gladys went away disappointed, but not deterred from her goal. She would find some way to act upon God's Word. Obtaining a job as a parlor maid in a wealthy woman's house, she determined to save her money until she had enough to buy her own ticket to China.

Arriving at her new place of employment, Gladys went to her tiny bedroom and sat on the edge of the bed. Reaching for her suitcase, she pulled out her Bible. Opening it, she placed the few pennies she had on top of it, and prayed, "O God, here's my Bible! Here's my money! Here I am. Use me, God!"

A knock came at her door. Another maid was there with the message that the lady of the house wanted to see her. Going downstairs, Gladys met her new mistress.

"I always pay the fare of my maids," she said, handing Gladys three shillings.

Gladys added this unexpected money to her pennies and praised the Lord. After many months Gladys had enough money for a train ticket to Vladivostok on the Trans-Siberian Railroad. From there she went by boat and mule to Yangcheng, China.

The woman had no money and no supporters but God. She was there not because someone had sent her but because she had acted upon God's command to go! His Word was enough for her.[5]

What is God asking you to do for Him right now, at this stage in your life? He probably won't ask you to go to China,

Mongolia, or Tibet. He might not even call upon you to take up prison reform or fly a helicopter in Africa. But He does have something He wants you to do. Search the Word until you find out what it is. Then with a willing heart act upon that Word.

## A Woman of Action

References: Esther 1-10; *Prophets and Kings,* pp. 598-606.

1. **When?**
   a. How many years do the events in the book of Esther cover? (Dates appear in reference Bibles.)
   b. Compare the dates with those of other Bible books. Which books cover a similar time period?
   c. What other Bible characters might Esther and Mordecai have known or had knowledge of?
   d. The Jews to this day celebrate the feast of Purim, Esther's feast day, to commemorate the deliverance. It is held the fourteenth and fifteenth days of Adar, the twelfth month in the Jewish calendar, approximately our March.

2. **Where?**
   a. Using the maps in a reference Bible or Bible atlas, locate Shushan and the Medo-Persian Empire.
   b. Compare with modern maps of the Middle East. In what country is Shushan (Susa) now located?

3. **Who?**
   a. Make a list of the main characters and jot down indications of their personality and character.
   b. What emotions did Esther face in each scene in this dramatic story? List the scenes, characters, and emotions.

4. **What?**
   a. What problem did Esther have to solve?
   b. What indications do you have that Esther had the following:
      i. The basis for doing.
      ii. The heart for doing.
      iii. The act of doing.
   c. What actions did she take? List each action.

87

        i. To prepare to go before the king.
        ii. To enlist the king to help her people.
     d. What indications are there that God was in control of
        the situation?
5. **Why?**
     a. Why do you think Esther was willing to risk her life?
     b. Why do you think Scripture included this story?
     c. What message does this story have for you?

## PERSONAL DISCOVERIES

1. Read through the book of Esther, writing a title of no more than 10 words for each chapter. If Esther were to be told as a modern adventure story of love and palace intrigue, what title do you think would sell the book?

2. Read the following texts. How do they illustrate the truth of this chapter? How does the story of Esther illustrate these texts? James 2:12-18; 1 John 3:17, 18; Matthew 25:31-46; Titus 1:16; Galatians 5:6.

3. From your library or a Christian bookstore get a copy of Charles M. Sheldon's *In His Steps*. Republished after a half century, it is the story of a woman whose life changed when she surrendered to the Word of God and actually began to do what the Bible says.

## GROUP DISCOVERIES

1. Mordecai was the most influential person in Esther's life. He gave her spiritual training, counsel, direction, and challenge. Whom would you name as the strongest spiritual influence in your life? Why?

2. Brainstorm about women in the Bible who had strength of character, were willing to take risks, to act courageously—women of faith and action. Who would be in your Hall of Fame?

3. What does the story of Esther reveal to you about the character of God? Give incidents to illustrate each trait you mention. Write them down in two columns on a board or large sheet of paper. Label one column "God Is . . ."; label the other "As Shown by . . ."

    [1] Lois Dick, "Summoned by the Thunderbolt," *Signs of the Times,* December 1988.

[2] K. Bartalsky, *Soaring on Broken Wings,* pp. 79-85.

[3] L. Sotnak, *Their Light Still Shines,* pp. 86-91.

[4] Dick, "A Fire Aflame in Tibet," *Signs of the Times,* November 1988.

[5] A. Burgess, *The Small Woman,* pp. 16-61.

*12*

# The Power for Doing

I have often struggled to have an obedient heart. One of those battles occurred at a women's retreat. The presenter had asked us to think of someone who had hurt us in life. "Make a list of your hurts," she said. "When you are ready, take your list to the fire and burn it. This act will symbolize your choice to let go of your pain."

For a long while I stared at my list. Others were going to the fire, but I could not. I wasn't even sure that I wanted to give up those injuries. Finally I went to my room and got on my knees. "I can't, Lord. I can't do it!"

"Give your hurts to Me, Dorothy," He whispered to my heart. "Forgive that person, as I have forgiven you."

"You'll have to help me," I replied. I stood then, and headed for the fire. God's power propelled me. I threw in my list and watched it burst into flame. Taking a deep breath, I felt new life. What I could not do myself He had done for me.

This is the good news! God will do for us what we cannot do for ourselves. He alone can supply the power for our doing.

## HE SUPPLIES THE POWER

The truth of the matter is that we cannot do the Word, but if we have a willing heart and step out in faith, then the Lord comes forward and does for us, works in us. "For it is God which worketh in you both to will and to do of his good pleasure" (Phil. 2:13).

Doing the Word is all grace, allowing God to do for us what we cannot do for ourselves.

Sarah experienced God's gracious supplying of power. Engaged to a man who was not a believer, she knew that God's Word counseled against such unions, but she felt helpless to break it off. She shared her problem with a friend, Catherine Marshall.

"I love Jeb so much. He's just what I've always wanted," Sarah began, love shining in her eyes. "Except for one thing—he isn't a Christian and seems to have no interest in God. Sometimes I wonder if God is telling me to break my engagement."

"What makes you think that?" Catherine asked.

Tears glistened in Sarah's eyes. "I don't think I could hold on to my faith and Jeb, too. As much as I love Jeb, my relationship with God is even more precious. Thanks, Catherine; I think I know what I need to do."

"And what's that?" Catherine encouraged.

"I'm going to break the engagement. It will be hard, but with God's help I'll do it. Pray for me."

God supplied the power for Sarah to follow through with her commitment. A year later Sarah wrote to Catherine, "It nearly killed me to give up Jeb. Yet God knew that he wasn't the one for me. Recently I've met a wonderful Christian man. We're going to be married. I'm so thankful I trusted God." [1]

When we do what we *can* do—choose to obey—then God comes forward and does His part. "The power of choice that God has given to [women]; it is theirs to exercise. You cannot change your heart, . . . but you can *choose* to serve Him. You can give Him your will; He will then work in you to will and to do according to His good pleasure." [2]

CHOOSING GOD'S POWER

Jami Breedlove, who had been raised in a Bible-believing home, grew up with homosexual desires that she at first fought, then accepted as the way she had to be. She lived openly as a lesbian for 12 years, but struggled to find peace with God.

As hard as she tried, she couldn't validate her lifestyle with God's Word. Whenever she prayed, she thought of a passage from 1 Corinthians 6:9 that listed homosexual behavior among the sins that would prevent people from entering heaven. She got out her Bible and read it over and over. Then one day she noticed verse 11, which proclaimed, "And that is what some of you were. But you were washed, you were sanctified, you were justified in the name of the Lord Jesus Christ and by the Spirit of our God" (NIV).

*Is this saying that God can change what I am?* Jami wondered. *I guess I have to make a choice here. Either I can continue to choose my lesbian lifestyle, or I can take a chance God can change my life and perfect my heterosexuality, which I believe is His purpose for my life.*

Jami made her choice based on God's Word. She broke off the homosexual relationship. It was a wrenching experience. But she eventually married an understanding Christian man whom God helped her to love and to enjoy sexually.

After living as a heterosexual for nine years, she testifies, "God *can* change a homosexual's heart. I know, because I've experienced it. . . . Obeying God is a choice we make every day. My husband can choose to commit heterosexual adultery. . . . I can choose to do the same toward a man or a woman. But when there have been occasions . . . for me to walk in disobedience, I always turn around, align myself with the Word of God, and say no. I choose God because His way is better."[3]

PROMISES OF POWER

The issue is different for each of us. For some it may be chemical addictions, for others temperance in work habits. Some struggle with sexual issues, while others deal with relationship problems. Many fight against a call to service, and others struggle with dishonesty. The devil has sin packaged in all sizes, shapes, and colors, but it is always something that goes against God's will. No matter what our private challenge of obedience to the Word may be, God has promised all the power we need to do it.

A promise I discovered one morning filled me with joy and hope. "How awesome you are, O God. . . . You are the One who gives power and strength to your people. . . . Praise to our God!" (Ps. 68:35, Clear Word).

I am not able, but He *is* able. I am weak, but He *is* strong. I feel helpless, but He has all power in heaven and earth. And that power is mine. "When the soul, realizing its helplessness, reaches out after Christ, He will reveal Himself in power."[4]

Once I struggled with anger and bitterness toward a certain couple. Because the wife had spread false reports about my husband, I began to hate them. But the Word of God came to me: "Love your enemies, bless them that curse you, do good to them that hate you, and pray for them which despitefully use you" (Matt. 5:44).

I felt so helpless to do this. I prayed, "Lord, please, I want to obey Your Word, but it isn't in me to do it!"

"Do the acts of love," the Lord nudged me as I talked with Him. "I'll work for you."

So I chose to obey, setting about to do the actions of love. God gave me courage to write a note, to bring them a little gift, to greet them warmly. I acted the Word of God to love them even though I didn't feel like it. God took away the hate and gave me love instead. He supplied the power for me to do all that He had asked. Then He gave me the feeling as well!

## THE PATHWAY OF OBEDIENCE

In this section we have talked about four markers on the path to obedience: the basis, the heart, the act, and the power. The story of Sheila Walsh, gospel singer, illustrates these markers.

**The basis.** Sheila tells about the time when she wanted to divorce her husband. He hadn't been unfaithful. Theirs was a survival marriage, two people living together without real love and intimacy. Miserable, she looked for a way out.

She went to see a Christian friend, told him how she was feeling, and asked him to confront her with eternal, biblical truth. Many friends agreed she should leave Norman. But what did God have to say about it? Sheila sought out the authoritative Word of God, which must be the basis of all doing.

**The heart.** She didn't like what she found in God's Word, but decided to obey it anyway. Being willing was the hard part. "Once you decide to do something God's way you don't suddenly feel wonderful. For me it took months to restore a sense of peace and excitement, to look forward to the future."

**The act.** The next thing Sheila faced was the need for action.

About this time she read a book about spiritual warfare. For the first time she realized that Satan was attempting to destroy her life, her ministry, and her marriage. "I put the book down and said to the enemy, 'I know who you are. I know what you're trying to do. But the victory has already been won in Jesus Christ.'"

Then she realized she needed to put on God's armor so that she might live victoriously, and began nurturing her relationship with God in the mornings. Her plan is to read a chapter or two from God's Word. She chooses one verse to memorize, then meditates on it as she walks, asking God to speak through that verse and give her power for her day.

**The power.** God began to work in Sheila's and Norman's lives. She testifies, "Now it's so great to tell people that God is faithful and know that it is true. I can say that I never loved my husband as much as I do today." While she could not turn her marriage around, God did, because both she and her husband were willing to allow Him to work in them.[5]

Your situation may be very different. But whatever your challenge, God will give you power to do His will. God loves you as much as He loves Sarah, Jami, Sheila, or me. He can supply the power to make His Word a reality in your life.

### Our Part, God's Part
Read the texts. Fill in the information on the chart below.

| Text | Our Part | God's Part |
|------|----------|------------|
| 2 Kings 4:1-7 | | |
| 2 Chron. 20:14-27 | | |
| Luke 8:43-48 | | |
| John 11:39-44 | | |
| John 2:7-9 | | |
| John 6:9-13 | | |
| Mark 7:24-30 | | |

PERSONAL DISCOVERIES
    1. Do a study of the word "help" and its related words ("helped," "helper," "helping") in the book of Psalms. Thirty-seven psalms contain the word. In five "help" appears twice:

Psalms 40, 46, 70, 118, 121. Two repeat it three times: Psalms 22 and 119. Read one psalm each day, giving special study to the verses with the word "help" in them. Notice the many situations in which God is able and willing to aid us.

2. Parallelism is one device used by the Hebrew poets. Read a bit of Psalm 22. Notice how many of the verses are couplets. Sometimes the second statement is just another way of expressing the same thing as the first. Occasionally the first is a question and the second an answer. Or the two statements may be in contrast to each other. Write a prayer psalm, asking God for help, strength, and power to act according to His Word. Use the Hebrew poetic form to write nonrhyming couplets that express your own cry for help.

3. Consider the following stories of Bible women we have already studied in detail: widow of Zarephath (1 Kings 17); Hagar (Gen. 16:1-16; 21:1-21); woman with the issue of blood (Luke 8:43-48); Hannah (1 Sam. 1, 2). See if you can pinpoint each of the four markers on the pathway of obedience in each woman's story.

    a. The basis of doing.

    b. A heart for doing.

    c. The act of doing.

    d. The power for doing.

GROUP DISCOVERIES

1. Share a time that God helped you to obey His Word despite the fact that you felt unable to do it on your own. Tell about a time that you yielded to His will, stepped out in faith, and He did for you what you could not do for yourself.

2. Make a list of battles in the Old Testament in which the outcome seemed hopeless to God's people—times that nothing happened until they obeyed God's command and stepped out in faith. (Example: Red Sea.) Try to list 10 such incidents.

3. How has the Spirit been speaking to you during these "Doing the Word" studies? Have you made any changes in your life as a result of these Bible studies? What changes do you believe God wants you to make in your actions this coming week?

---

[1] Catherine Marshall, *Adventures in Prayer* (New York: Ballantine Books, 1976), pp. 53, 54.

[2] E. G. White, *Steps to Christ,* pp. 47, 48.

[3] Jami Breedlove, "I Left My Lesbian Lifestyle," *Today's Christian Woman,* March/April, 1995.

[4] White, *Steps to Christ,* p. 65.

[5] Rebecca K. Grosenbach, "Free to Be . . . Sheila Walsh," *Today's Christian Woman,* September/October 1989.

*13*

# Fixing Priorities

Corrie ten Boom was standing with hundreds of other poorly clad women. Around them rose high concrete walls topped with barbed wire. They were waiting for roll call at Ravensbruck concentration camp during World War II.

At last the camp officials ordered the newly arrived women to turn in their possessions, then walk naked past the guards for inspection. The camp wanted to make sure that they smuggled nothing in with them.

*No! I can't give up my Bible!* Corrie thought. *And Betsie needs the one sweater we have and the vitamin drops. Lord, what can I do? I know, I'll ask to use the toilet!*

A guard stood nearby. "Where are the toilets?" she asked. He nodded his head toward the shower room. "Use the drain holes."

Once inside, Corrie scanned the abandoned room for a hiding place. In a corner stood a stack of benches. Quickly she wrapped the Bible and vitamin drops in the sweater and stuffed it behind the benches. Then she hurried back to her place in line.

They stripped, were given prison dresses, and told to shower. After a hurried shower Corrie put on the thin dress. No one seemed to notice as she retrieved her bundle. She hung the Bible in its little bag from a string around her neck and, lifting her dress, tied the sweater around her waist.

*I'll never pass inspection!* Corrie shook her head. *The bulge is obvious, and you can see right through these dresses.* She sent a prayer to heaven and took her place in line.

The guards ran their hands down the bodies of each woman, checking for smuggled goods. They inspected the woman in front of Corrie three times but seemed not to notice Corrie as she walked untouched past them.

She encountered a second line. The woman guard shoved Corrie ahead. "Move along! You're too slow!"

Eventually Corrie reached Barracks 28 and found a place for her and her sister Betsie on one of the straw-covered platforms. The place was crawling with fleas. In fact, it was so bad that no guard would enter Barracks 28, although they inspected every other barracks daily. This gave Corrie and Betsie complete freedom to read their Bible, not only for themselves but for dozens of women who came to their daily Bible reading.

The Word was precious to those women! Treasuring the moments they could spend reading its message each day, they worked hard to finish their quota of knitting so that they would have a few more minutes with the Word. Those women truly desired the Word of God. To them it was "more to be desired than gold, yea, than much fine gold." It was their most valued possession; to read it was their greatest desire.[1]

Using the letters of the word D-E-S-I-R-E as an acrostic, I'll share with you some things I've learned from Christian women who have desired the Word the way I want to desire the Word. *D*ecide what is most important; *E*liminate the unessential; *S*chedule time with the Word; *I*nvest in that which strengthens the desire; *R*epetition forms the habit; *E*steem the Word above all else.

## D—DECIDE WHAT IS MOST IMPORTANT

Fay Angus's most treasured possession was a stuffed toy. Just 12 years old when taken to a labor camp in China with her mother, she was allowed by the occupying soldiers only whatever personal items she could carry. The girl begged to take her favorite stuffed animal, Dog Toby. She loved the little dog with his shoe-button eyes and embroidered mouth.

Her mother agreed, then took out the stuffing and replaced it with what she considered important—tight wads of Chinese paper money. Into the skinny tail she crammed British pound notes. Then Fay walked right by the inspection guards, Dog Toby under her arm.

However, they were unable to use the worthless money, and Dog Toby didn't have any answers for a teenager's hard questions about the cruelties of war. What they had thought important was, in the end, of little value. But before Fay left that camp she had come face-to-face with God's Word shared by a fellow prisoner. In it she found eternal value, that which gave her hope and a reason to live. She went into the camp with one treasure, but came out with one far more valuable.[2]

### E—Eliminate the Unessential

Colleen Townsend Evans, former Hollywood star, has been a busy pastor's wife for many years. At one point she was so involved in raising children, church activities, and community projects that she was at the point of a breakdown in her health.

She refused when the doctor ordered her to a hospital. Who was going to care for her responsibilities? she asked.

"You are trying to be a superwife, a supermom, and a superfriend to the whole community," her doctor countered. "I know how much you want to serve the Lord and the whole world, but if you keep this up, you won't be able to serve anybody!"

That night in the quietness of her home Colleen poured out her heart to the Lord. "God, guide me. Show me how to live. Tell me what I must cut out of my schedule. Lord, please, with all my heart, I want You to become the Lord of my daily routine."

When Christ did become Lord of her daily routine, He took away her need to be a superwoman. He taught her to say no to people so that she might say yes to Him.

"If you are caught," Colleen writes, "as I was, in the barrenness of a too-busy life, look to Jesus. The Gospels reveal Him as a man who had learned the importance of saying no."[3]

I had never thought of Jesus in quite that light before. It revealed something to me of His humanity, this idea of a God who needed to say no because He was "in all points tempted as we are." In His strength, I too can learn to say no.

## S—Schedule Time With the Word

Elizabeth Dole, a woman who has served her government as secretary of transportation and later as secretary of labor, resigned in 1990 to become the first female president of the American Red Cross since Clara Barton. She is a career woman who has learned to schedule time with the Word.

Once at a prayer breakfast she talked about the need to eliminate the unessentials from life in order to focus on what is truly important—a relationship with Jesus Christ. She confessed her own problems with priorities. As a result she found herself facing spiritual starvation. Something had to change!

Elizabeth gave up some responsibilities. She joined a weekly Bible study group and began to put time with God as the number one priority in her life, scheduling her devotions for the early morning before her husband gets up.[4]

In the next chapter, "Finding the Time," we will meet other women who schedule time with God's Word, and we'll discover some practical ideas of how to do it ourselves.

## I—Invest in Those Things That Strengthen Your Desire

If we really desire the Word, if it is the most important consideration in our lives, then we will find the money and the time to invest in that which will strengthen that desire. We will find a way to get the tools we need to enrich our Bible study.

For example, we will discover how to attend special retreats, convocations, and seminars that will help us understand God's Word better. Doing without other conveniences or pleasures, we will put our time and our money where our treasure is!

## R—Repetition Forms the Habit

A few years ago, after an accident, Ruth Bell Graham experienced memory loss as a result of a concussion. She was unable to remember a single Bible verse.

Alarmed, she cried out to God, "Take anything I have, but please give me back my Bible verses."

Immediately Jeremiah 31:3 came to mind: "I have loved thee with an everlasting love: therefore with lovingkindness have I drawn thee." She didn't remember when she had memorized it, but there it was in answer to her prayer. Other verses came back one by one. "That experience made me realize what a treasure those Bible verses are!" she says.[5]

In chapter 15 we will discuss ways to memorize Scripture and the importance of filling our minds with gems from the treasure chest of God's Word.

Is God's Word so important to you that you could pray "Lord, take anything I have—my sight, my hearing, my taste, the use of my hands or my feet—but please, please, give me back my Bible verses, my most valued treasure"?

### E—ESTEEM THE WORD ABOVE ALL ELSE

I challenge you to pursue the presence of God until His Word becomes to you more than food and better than gold; until it has the highest spot in your affections; until you value it more than anything else in life.

Bibles were scarce in Wales in 1794. The available few were so expensive that only the wealthy could afford one. The Jones family was poor, but that did not stop Mary from pursuing God's presence in His Word.

One day she walked two miles to a neighbor's home and timidly asked, "Please, may I read your Bible for just a little while?"

"Of course, my child," the farmer's wife replied. "Come in." She led Mary into the best room of the house, where the Bible sat in a place of honor. Then she quietly slipped out, leaving the girl alone with a Bible for the first time in her life.

Breathless with excitement, Mary lifted the cloth covering the Bible and placed it on the table beside her. With trembling hands she opened the large Book. By chance it fell open to John 5. There she read the words of Jesus: "Search the scriptures; for in them ye think ye have eternal life: and they are they which testify of me" (verse 39).

"I will! I will!" she cried. "Oh, if only I had a Bible of my own!"

Six years later Mary walked barefoot 28 miles to the town of Bala, where Welsh Bibles were for sale. In her pocket was the money she had saved. She went straight to the home of Pastor

Thomas Charles, who had the only copies then available.

"I'm so sorry," Pastor Charles explained. "All of the Bibles I have are already reserved."

Unable to believe the news, she began to cry as if her heart would break. "I wanted one so much! I've worked hard for six years and saved all my money. I've walked here 28 miles to get one, and now you tell me there aren't any left?"

Tears filled the pastor's eyes as well. "You shall have a Bible," he said, handing her one of his reserved copies.

Two years later Mr. Charles told Mary's story in London and pleaded for a society to be formed to print and circulate Welsh Bibles.

"Why for Wales only?" someone else suggested. "Why not for the whole world?"

So it was that because of Mary's desire for the Word of God the British and Foreign Bible Society formed on March 7, 1804. Today most people can get a Bible in their own language. I'm sure you have one. Will you not determine to treasure it above everything else you own?[6]

SEARCH THE WORD

### Mary's Desire

References: Luke 10:38-42; *The Desire of Ages,* pp. 524, 525.

1. Observation

   a. Bethany was the home of Mary, Martha, and Lazarus. What facts about Bethany, its location, how often Jesus visited, the main events that occurred there, etc., can you gather from reading the following texts? Make a list of the facts you discover. John 11:18; Mark 11:11; Matthew 21:17; John 11:5; Luke 24:50, 51.

   b. Do a personality study of Mary and Martha. Make two columns on a piece of paper. Sort the following words into the proper column under one of the sisters' names: quiet, studious, active, anxious, loving, affectionate, impulsive, outspoken, impatient, sensitive, bold, shy, a doer, a thinker, a hard worker, a good listener, bossy, easily led, devoted, understanding, organized, reverent, perplexed, frustrated, courteous, careful, troubled, pushy, retiring, extrovert, introvert, sanguine, choleric, melancholy, phlegmatic, believing, trusting, complaining, assertive, peaceful, jealous, selfish, joyous, zealous, diligent, prompt, energetic, calm, devotional spirit, contemplative mind. Add any other descriptive words that come to your mind.

2. **Interpretation**
   a. Why did Jesus enjoy going to Mary and Martha's home?
   b. What was "that good part" that Mary had chosen?
   c. What was the "one thing" that Martha needed?
   d. Why do you think Jesus said what He did to Martha? How do you think she responded?

3. **Application**
   a. Are you more like Mary or Martha in the following areas?
      i. Spiritual priorities.
      ii. Relational skills.
      iii. On the job.
      iv. At home.
      v. In temperament.
   b. If Jesus came to your house to spend a day or two, what would be three changes He would recommend you make in regard to your habits and activities?

PERSONAL DISCOVERIES

1. Read the following texts:. Matthew 6:33; John 17:1-3; 4:14; Psalm 73:24-26; Jeremiah 15:16; Psalm 19:8-11; 42:1, 2; Matthew 16:26; 5:6. Which texts best suit Martha? Mary? Choose the one that best expresses your need right now. Paraphrase it as your message from God for this day.

2. Read John 11:17-43. Which of the sisters showed greater faith on this occasion? Do you see any connection between the sisters' behavior at the tomb and their experience recorded in Luke 10?

3. Do a brief analysis of the feast at Simon's house as recorded in John 12:1-8. Use one of the methods outlined in chapter 3. What more do you learn about Mary and her relationship to Jesus?

## GROUP DISCOVERIES

1. Imagine that you were suddenly reduced to dire poverty. What things in your possession or lifestyle would you struggle hardest to preserve? Why are they important to you? List 12 to 15 items. Now go back and cross out all but the five most important. Share your final list with your group.

2. Ask the group to make a list of five things they have to do tomorrow. Put them in order, most important to least important. Let the members of the group share lists. Did they put "time with the Word" as a high priority item?

3. Can you think of a time when you realized that God's Word was more precious to you than anything else in life? Share with the group.

4. List other Bible women who desired the Word—the Living Word or the Written Word. What is the basis for including them on a roster of women who treasured the Word?

---

[1] C. ten Boom, *The Hiding Place*, pp. 172-184.

[2] Marjorie Chandler, "A POW's Season to Survive," *Virtue*, November/December 1991.

[3] V. Z. Bright, ed., *The Greatest Lesson I've Ever Learned*, pp. 78-85.

[4] J. Woodbridge, *More Than Conquerors*, pp. 45-48.

[5] James Schaffer and Colleen Todd, *Christian Wives* (Garden City, N.J.: Doubleday and Co., Inc., 1987), pp. 52-55.

[6] Dorothy Eaton Watts, *This Is the Day* (Hagerstown, Md.: Review and Herald Publishing Assn., 1982), p. 74.

*14*

# Finding
# the Time

"You need to spend time with God every day," Becky Tirabassi told her Bible study class.

*Becky, you're a hypocrite,* her conscience prodded. *You don't practice what you preach. You are so busy serving God that you are spending only two or three minutes a day with the Lord.*

It was true. Becky *was* busy. A wife and the mother of a toddler, she led three Bible study groups weekly and coached the cheerleaders at the local high school. In her special ministry of witnessing to high school students, she traveled the country telling her conversion story.

Becky had fallen into the trap many of us are in—God's work takes so much time we have no time for God Himself. She determined to adjust her priorities, but didn't know how to find the time.

Shortly after that Becky attended a seminar on prayer at which she made a commitment to pray one hour every day. That was in 1984, and she has kept that vow ever since. She quotes Corrie ten Boom as saying, "Don't pray when you feel like it. Make an appointment with the King." Becky began doing just that. She wrote in her prayer hour every day on her calendar.

## SCHEDULED TIME

Becky Tirabassi got her priorities in order, made a commitment, then scheduled that time into her day. It meant spending less time watching TV at night so she could go to bed early and get up one hour sooner. Most of all, it meant not allowing anything else to crowd out that hour, but she testifies that it has been worth it.

"When I began to eliminate some of the busyness in my life and focus on the gifts God has given me," she writes, "I began to accomplish more. I learned to say no a lot more. For instance, instead of taking on more work, I began to delegate. . . . [I've been] continually trying to adjust to what I feel God is showing me was important in a particular season of my life."

Becky has a plan to take her through her one hour with the Lord. She reads from the Old Testament, the New Testament, and the book of Proverbs every day. Also she keeps a prayer notebook in which she writes down the messages God gives her as she reads. Then she writes her prayers in another part of the notebook.[1]

Margaret Cundiff of Yorkshire, England, is a professional woman who finds she must write "Time With God" into one of the slots in her daily appointment book. If she doesn't do it, she finds the spaces get filled with urgent tasks until she has no time left for God and His Word. She came to this practice after discovering one day that her schedule book was filled with the names of people, many of them strangers, to whom she was giving part of her day, but that she was spending no time at all with the One she loved most. Scheduling has made a big difference in Margaret's life.[2]

Susanna Wesley was not content with meeting God once a day. She set aside three periods of meditation and reflection on God's Word daily. Although the mother of John and Charles Wesley and 16 other children, the wife of a preacher, and an active spiritual leader in her own right, she insisted upon the discipline of three quiet times with the Lord every day![3]

Debbie Boone also has scheduled regular time with God into her day. Right now it's early morning, but she's finding it hard when she gets to bed late at night. "I'm starting to question whether that's my time of day or not," she writes. "Maybe it's evening, and I just have to drop all the things I try to get done after everybody is in bed. I'm sort of juggling right now. But if morning is the only time I can find, then I get up at six and have my hour before anyone else is up."[4]

## WAITING TIME

Joyce Rogers has discovered "waiting times" to be wonderful chances to spend time with God. One day she took stock of some of the times when she has to wait: red lights, stop signs, the doctor's office, the dentist's office, the beauty parlor, supermarket checkout lines, bank lines, and times her husband is late for a meal.

If she's home waiting, she likes to sit at the piano and employ the time to sing praises to God. She carries Scripture cards with her in the car, using them to memorize verses while waiting at red lights or in traffic jams. And she always takes her Bible with her to the doctor's office or to the beauty parlor.

"This strategy helps me focus on God rather than on my circumstances," Joyce declares. "Waiting on others can remind us to wait on Him. Instead of becoming impatient, I find myself looking forward to those times."[5]

Ruth Bell Graham tells about a time she was in the high school infirmary for a whole day. She used that time to read through the entire book of Psalms. "When I got through it," she says, "I felt as though there was a glow in the room."[6]

Both Joyce and Ruth put into practice the suggestion of Ellen White: "Keep your Bible with you. As you have opportunity, read it; fix the texts in your memory. Even while you are walking the streets you may read a passage and meditate upon it, thus fixing it in the mind."[7]

## MAKING TIME

Once Audrey Wetherell Johnson taught a Bible study class for factory girls in England. She urged them to have a morning time for prayer and reading the Bible.

Gladys tried it and reported her experience at the next meeting. "We sleep 12 in our bed! I got out early and tried to kneel, and my brothers threw their boots at me, so I can't do it!" The other girls nodded. It seemed impossible to find a quiet spot in their crowded apartments to be alone with God.

"Gladys, God created you to love you and for you to get to know Him by reading about Him," Audrey replied. "I know God wants you to spend time with Him. As to how or when, you ask Him, and He will help you find a place and a time."

At the next meeting, the girl reported finding an open church at lunchtime, where she could go in to read and pray without disturbance.[8]

I sympathize with Gladys. There have been times, especially when the children were still at home, that it was difficult to find a quiet time or spot to be alone with God and His Word. I had to make an effort to find an occasion and a place. At different times I remember going for a walk to be alone with God, of taking my Bible to a corner of the garden to study, or of retreating to a quiet corner of a public library. I know from experience that if we want that time with God badly enough, we will find the occasion and the place to make it happen.

Anne Ortlund sometimes goes to a quiet corner of a restaurant where she knows no one. There she has breakfast, plans, reads, and writes out her prayers. In good weather she drives to a scenic spot to have her devotions. She has even gone to a couch in a secluded nook of a hotel lobby.[9]

Mary Irwin, widow of astronaut Jim Irwin, remembers how he had a reading rack attached to his exercise bicycle so that during his morning physical workouts he could feed his mind on God's Word. In this way he read through the whole Bible every year.[10]

Ruth Bell Graham leaves an open Bible on the coffee table. That way, when she has spare moments she can read a verse or two and relax. She also memorizes verses as she drives, irons, washes dishes, or does other household tasks.[11]

Evelyn Christenson, author of several books on prayer, doesn't have all the time she wants to spend meditating on God's Word. So she tries to keep the radio and TV turned off during the day. This eliminates distractions and allows her to meditate on what she has studied as she goes about her work. She also keeps her prayer notebook nearby so that when thoughts come to her, wherever she is, she can stop a moment and write down what God is saying to her.[12]

I travel a lot—with my husband around the conference, and in airplanes to speaking appointments at camp meetings and women's retreats. My Bible and journal go along in my briefcase. I've had some wonderful times with God's Word in motel rooms, air terminal waiting lounges, and on long flights across the country. Also, my journal helps me to make the most of the moments I can find to spend with God.

## PRAYING FOR TIME

Emilie Barnes was a young mother with two toddlers of her own plus three others she was caring for day and night. She was at the point of exhaustion. It seemed she was washing, ironing, pot-tying, diapering, and feeding 24 hours a day with not a minute to herself, let alone time for God.

"What can I do, Lord?" she cried out one afternoon. "I can't handle this! I need time!"

Emilie thought she heard God speaking to her. "You could get up early in the morning when the house is quiet."

"OK, Lord," Emilie agreed, "but I can't do this unless You help me find the time. I just have too many things to do in a day to add Bible reading!"

She set her alarm at 4:50 each morning, realizing that she'd have to do this before anybody else got up or the demands of the day intruded. Emilie soon saw God doing something wonderful for her. Not only did He help her to wake up each morning, He helped her to get organized so that she could save time on her chores.

"God met my need every day," Emilie declares. Whereas before she had no time, God helped her to find time, not only for His Word, but to write books to share with other struggling mothers what she had learned.[13]

When Anne Ortlund had three babies under 2½, one of them a newborn, she prayed, "Lord, if You'll help me, I'll meet You from 2:00 to 3:00 a.m." Looking back, she comments, "I didn't die; and I'm not sorry I did it. Everybody has 24 hours. We can soak ourselves in prayer, in His Word, in Himself, if we really want to."[14]

I remember two times when my schedule had become over-loaded and I felt too stressed out to spend quality time in study of the Word. I wrote in my journal, "Lord, I need more days in this month! Please give me the gift of more time!"

On both occasions someone phoned to cancel a program at which I was scheduled to speak. Other times God shows me what I need to eliminate so that I have the time. Or He provides help through friends or makes tasks go much easier than I had anticipated. When I ask the Lord to help me find time, He does.

## THE HABIT OF FINDING TIME

Like any other habit of life, pursuing God's presence gets easier the more we do it. Doing something over and over forms a pathway in our brains. Done often enough an action can become automatic. Once a regular devotional time has been established, you'll find yourself longing for it, hungry for it.

Just as we get used to eating at certain times every day, and our stomach lets us know if we are late, so will our spiritual nature crave the set time we have with God and His Word. So I urge you to hang in there until pursuing God's presence becomes more important to you than your daily food.

Ruth Bell Graham has made such a habit of pursuing God's presence through the Word that she has worn out six Bibles. They actually fell apart from constant handling. Her seventh shows much use.

Recently a friend brought her a roll of transparent tape. She squealed with delight, "Wonderful! Oh, thank you so much!" It was a special kind available only in England, a kind that Ruth uses to repair the torn pages of her Bible.[15]

Could you leaf through her Bible, you would find pages worn through from use. Notes are scattered in the margins. Here and there the edges are ripped. With her special tape she can repair those pages.

What does your Bible look like? Is it falling apart from daily use, or is it as crisp and new as the day you got it 10 or 20 years ago? The daily habit of finding time for God's Word will wear it out. Guaranteed!

## SEARCH THE WORD
### Lydia Found Time
References: Acts 16; *The Acts of the Apostles,* pp. 211-220.
1. **Who?**
Use your Bible, *The Seventh-day Adventist Bible Commentary,* a Bible dictionary, or an encyclopedia of the Bible to verify the following facts about Lydia. Can you learn any other details of her life?

a. A wealthy businesswoman trading in purple dye made of madder root.

b. She pursued the presence of God, finding time in spite of her busy career.

c. She was the first Christian convert in Europe.

d. She was named after the province in Asia from which she came, a province famous for trade throughout the Greco-Roman world.

e. Her cloth may have decorated Babylonian temples and clothed Roman emperors.

f. She was a Gentile who already worshiped the true God.

g. She likely belonged to the dyers' guild of Thyatira.

2. **When?**

a. Find the approximate dates for this story.

b. Name some contemporaries of Lydia. From Acts 15 and the book of Philippians make a list of four Christian missionaries and at least five Philippian church members that Lydia knew—two women and three men (one known by title only).

3. **Where?**

Use your Bible study resources to verify:

a. Location of places mentioned in Acts 16.

b. Philippi was on the great east-west Via Egnatia connecting Rome with Asia.

c. The name of the river where the women met to pray.

4. **Why?**

a. Why do you think Lydia's story is included in Scripture?

b. If you could go out to lunch with her, what advice might she give you about finding time for God and His Word?


PERSONAL DISCOVERIES

1. Study the book of Philippians carefully. Paul here lists his wishes and suggestions for Lydia and other Philippian Christians. Make a list of those wishes and admonitions. Check the ones that are needs you also have in your own spiritual life.

2. Make a list of women closely connected with Paul and his ministry. These texts may help: Acts 16; Acts 17:34; Acts 18; Acts 21:9; Romans 16:1, 2, 6, 12, 15; 1 Corinthians 1:11;

2 Timothy 1:5; 4:21; Philemon 1:2; Philippians 4:2. What snippets of information suggest to you that they were women devoted to the Word of God and pursuing the presence of Christ?

## GROUP DISCOVERIES

1. Let the group share ways in which they have found time for God and His Word.

2. The memory of the Sabbath that Paul came to the riverside prayer meeting was no doubt one that Lydia cherished all her life. When was the most memorable Sabbath in your own experience?

3. Why were the women meeting by the river, not in town?

[1] J. A. Talerico, "Becky Tirabassi: Keeping Her Balance."

[2] J. Lucas with C. Thom, *Friends of God,* pp. 74-83.

[3] Ruth A. Tucker, *First Ladies of the Parish* (Grand Rapids: Zondervan Publishing House, 1988), pp. 51-59.

[4] Dale Hanson Bourke, "How Does Debby Do It?" *Today's Christian Woman,* November/December 1990.

[5] V. Z. Bright, ed., *The Greatest Lesson I've Ever Learned,* pp. 146-148.

[6] Dale Hanson Bourke, "Ruth Bell Graham: Tough and Tender Moments," *Today's Christian Woman,* November/December 1991.

[7] E. G. White, *Steps to Christ,* p. 90.

[8] A. W. Johnson, *Created for Commitment,* p. 47.

[9] Anne Ortlund, *Disciplines of the Beautiful Woman* (Dallas: Word Publishing, 1984), p. 68.

[10] Lucas with Thom, p. 23.

[11] E. R. Skoglund, *Wounded Heroes,* pp. 194, 195.

[12] Debra Anne Bell, "Six Steps to Consistent Prayer," *Virtue,* May/June 1990.

[13] Dorothy Eaton Watts, *The Best You Can Be* (Hagerstown, Md.: Review and Herald Publishing Assn., 1993), pp. 88, 89.

[14] Ortlund, p. 29.

[15] Bourke.

# 15

# Filling the Mind

"Keedee! Keedee!" The harsh words of her captors and the sting of their sticks on her back kept Debbie moving along the rocky streambed.

Moments before, while on rounds in an Ethiopian mission hospital, Debbie Dortzbach had been taken at gunpoint by members of the Eritrean Liberation Front along with a Dutch nurse, Anna. A shot rang out. Debbie glanced over her shoulder and saw Anna fall. She wanted to go back, but her captors prodded her forward.

Expecting any moment to feel a bullet in her back, Debbie cried out, "How can I keep going, God? . . . I can't . . . I can't . . ." Tears blinded her eyes as she stumbled ahead.

They left the streambed and began climbing a steep cliff. Debbie looked up to the mountain range ahead. Suddenly words she had memorized long ago came back to her: "I will lift up my eyes to the hills—where does my help come from? My help comes from the Lord, the maker of heaven and earth."

The words filled her mind with hope and courage. "My help comes from the Lord!" Debbie repeated over and over as she resolutely placed one foot in front of the other, making herself keep up with her captors.

Later, when they stopped to make camp, Debbie repeated Psalm 91: "He who dwells in the shelter of the Most High will rest in the shadow of the Almighty. . . . I will say of the Lord,

'He is my refuge and my fortress, my God, in whom I trust!'"

This began a pattern of recalling Scripture that kept Debbie strong through 26 days of captivity while she was held for ransom by the terrorists.[1]

## WHY MEMORIZE SCRIPTURE?

I can think of at least five reasons for memorizing Scripture.

1. **Preparation for difficult times.** We never know when we will be in a situation such as Debbie's with no Bible in our possession. It is then that the truths hidden in our hearts will become our "shield" and our "buckler" (Ps. 91:4).

Looking forward to end-time events, we are told: "None but those who have fortified the mind with the truths of the Bible will stand through the last great conflict."[2] "In the time of great necessity [angels] will bring to [our] remembrance the very truths which are needed."[3]

Even now memorized Scripture will aid us during times of great stress. As the result of eye injuries from a car accident Edna Maye Gallington lay in a hospital under bright lights trying not to move. Her salvation was her store of Bible texts.

Many years before, she had typed favorite promises from each book of the Bible onto 3 x 5 cards that she kept beside her bed. Each night she read one or two of them. "Now lying in the emergency room," Edna wrote, "I let these encouraging, loving Bible statements wash through my mind, and I could feel the strength and peace they brought." The texts continued to bless her during the week she waited for the bandages to come off.[4]

2. **Protection against temptation.** "Thy word have I hid in mine heart," said David, "that I might not sin against thee" (Ps. 119:11). "Temptations often appear irresistible because . . . the tempted one cannot readily remember God's promises and meet Satan with the Scripture weapons."[5]

Elizabeth Mittelstaedt can testify to the truth of that statement. At a time of deep depression in her life, when standing on a bridge near Frankfurt, Germany, Satan came to her with the temptation to jump into the river.

At that very moment a scene from Matthew 4 came clearly to her mind, Jesus standing on the mountain and Satan telling Him to jump. She realized the source of her feelings and cried out to God for help. Scripture flashed in her mind at the appropriate moment, giving her the strength she needed to reach out for help.[6]

**3. Promotion of mental health.** "The entrance of thy word giveth light," says the psalmist (Ps. 119:130). It is one of the laws of the mind that it cannot hold on to two opposite ideas at the same time. It is possible to so fill our minds with joy and hope that it leaves no room for despondency and despair.

Sarah Fraser tells about a time of darkness when she cried out to God, "Help me!" Immediately she recalled a verse she had memorized when a young Christian: "Trust in the Lord with all thine heart; and lean not unto thine own understanding. In all thy ways acknowledge him, and he shall direct thy paths" (Prov. 3:5, 6).

*It is true that I have committed my way to the Lord, and I have acknowledged Him,* Sarah reasoned. *But then why am I so depressed? Where is God? Why isn't He helping me?*

She looked out the kitchen window and saw a cardinal perched on a lilac bush. For weeks she had seen nothing but starlings and crows. Now her spirit soared at the sight of gorgeous scarlet. The cardinal burst into song. Joy flooded her heart.

Her spirits revived, and hope returned. She still struggled with her problems, but she knew she had help. After that day Sarah resumed her daily time with God, asking Him to take her feelings and exchange them for His realities. She began replacing the stored gloom with bright promises of Scripture, reprogramming her subconscious mind. Sarah testifies that these scriptures had a large part in restoring her mental health.[7]

**4. Prompts spiritual growth and health.** "The habit [of memorizing texts] will prove a most valuable aid to religious growth,"[8] Ellen White says. "Desire the sincere milk of the word, that ye may grow thereby" (1 Peter 2:2).

Evelyn Harris discovered this principle early in life. Her mother took time every day to drill her on Bible verses. One of the passages was the Beatitudes, Matthew 5:3-12. As she repeated verse 6, "Blessed are they which do hunger and thirst after righteousness: for they shall be filled," Evelyn said she felt a strange stirring in her heart.

"That is God making you thirsty for Himself," Mother explained. "He is calling you to a new life in Christ Jesus."

Evelyn was baptized shortly after memorizing the text that initiated her spiritual birth. Throughout her life Bible verses tucked away in her heart kept her growing spiritually. She fed on them while walking the hills of South India as a missionary.[9]

**5. Pointers for daily living.** "Thy word is a lamp unto my feet," writes the psalmist, "and a light unto my path" (Ps. 119:105). Ellen White says it in a different way: "The memory must be filled with the precious truths of the Word. Then, like beautiful gems, these truths will flash out in the life."[10]

An example appears in the experience of Margaret Brand. At the time she was living at Vellore Medical College, where her husband was a surgeon working with the rehabilitation of lepers. One particular day while Dr. Brand was away from home, she noticed a ricksha stop and a young man head for their door. She could tell he was a leper.

"I'm sorry," Margaret told him. "Dr. Brand is out of town. He won't be back for several days."

The man nodded and turned to leave. By now the ricksha was gone. Margaret watched the leper hobble down the road. His shoulders sagged and he looked helpless and forlorn.

In that moment words stored in her memory pierced her thoughts: "I was a stranger, and ye took me in."

She called to him: "Wait! Do you have a place to stay?"

The leper shook his head. He had used his last money to hire the ricksha and had no friends with whom he could stay.

"Come stay with us," Margaret invited. "We'd be honored to have you as our guest!"

Dr. Brand was able to help Sadogopan, and he became a good friend. Margaret was thankful for God's Word that guided her that morning.[11]

### How to Memorize Scripture

**1. Outline it.** "Orderly words are attractive; they make learning easy," declares Florence Littauer. She advocates putting thoughts in outline form. We are to approach our memory assignment logically, looking for a pattern.[12] Follow natural divisions of the text. Here is an outline of James 1:19.

"Let every man be
swift to hear,
slow to speak,
slow to wrath."
The following outline of Matthew 7:7 is an acrostic as well.

**A**—"**A**sk, and it shall be given you;"

**S**—"**S**eek, and ye shall find;"

**K**—"**K**nock, and it shall be opened unto you."

Notice the natural progression of the verbs in Psalm 1:1.

"Blessed is the man that
*walketh* not in the counsel of the ungodly,
nor *standeth* in the way of sinners,
nor *sitteth* in the seat of the scornful."

Outlining helps you to understand what the verse says, and the form will help to fix it in your memory.

**2. Repeat it.** The more you do it, the easier it gets! "Though at first the memory be defective, it will gain strength by exercise, so that after a time you will delight thus to treasure up the words of truth," Ellen White reminds us.[13]

To establish a memory with easy recall, it is important to memorize over a period of time, occasionally reviewing what has been learned so that it can be brought up from the memory on demand.

**3. Use multiple senses.** Employ visual and kinesthetic senses as well as the auditory in your memorization work. Listening uses the auditory sense. Its effectiveness will increase if you repeat the text aloud. Looking at the text as you say it will add the visual sense, tripling the effect. Hearing the text, writing it, seeing it, and then verbalizing it is better yet.

Music and rhythm also help. "There are few means more effective for fixing His words in the memory than repeating them in song."[14] In referring to the thrice yearly journeys to Jerusalem for the feasts, Ellen White writes, "The songs that had cheered the wilderness wandering were sung. God's commandments were chanted, . . . and they were forever fixed in the memory."[15]

PRACTICAL SUGGESTIONS

1. Put memory texts on Post-It notes. Stick them around the house where you can see them often as you work.

2. Keep Scripture cards in your purse for waiting times.

3. Keep Scripture cards in the top drawer of your bedside table. Go over them when sleep evades you.

4. Books and tapes are available with Scripture set to music. Use them or make up your own tunes to fit the verses you choose.

5. Record Scripture passages. Listen to them as you work, jog, walk, or drive.

6. Use a text as the focal point of a creative art project.

7. Keep a notebook of promises you know. Review them occasionally.

## THE CATHEDRAL OF THE HEART

Darlene D. Rose spent four years in a prisoner-of-war camp in New Guinea during World War II. Often during those years she retreated, as she put it, to "the cathedral of [her] heart, and from His Word written upon the scroll of [her] memory" the Lord would read to her verses she had memorized long before.

One exceptionally dark night she sat with a group of Christians in a huddled circle for mutual encouragement. Darlene began quoting Psalm 27: "'The Lord is my light and my salvation; whom shall I fear? The Lord is the strength of my life; of whom shall I be afraid?'"

A hush fell over the group. A gentle wave of peace seemed to wash over them. The soft amens spoke of courage and faith. In that moment Darlene was thankful she had learned those words of hope. They had come back to her just when she needed them most.[16]

## SEARCH THE WORD
### Anna's Treasures
References: Luke 2:36-38; *The Desire of Ages,* pp. 50-58.
1. Observation
   a. Try to picture the scene in detail. What do you see, hear, smell, taste, feel?
   b. What was the law about purification? (Lev. 12).
   c. Write as many adjectives as possible to describe Anna.
2. Interpretation
   a. After a lifetime of looking for Christ's coming, what treasures do you think Anna may have stored in her memory?

Scan *The Desire of Ages,* pp. 1-50, for possibilities.

   b. As a prophet Anna would have been attracted to the Messianic psalms, Psalms 2, 22, 69, 72, 110. Which ones do you think she would have chosen to express her feelings on this day?

   c. Luke 2:38 says that Anna "spake of him to all them that looked for redemption in Jerusalem." What do you think she told people? Write her possible speech.

**3. Application**

   a. What message does Anna have for women living today?

   b. If you took Anna as a role model, how do you think her example would affect your lifestyle?

## PERSONAL DISCOVERIES

1. Anna was of the tribe of Aser, or Asher. Learn what you can about the history and character of this tribe. Try a Bible dictionary and these texts: Genesis 35:26; 46:17; 49:20; Deuteronomy 33:24; Numbers 1:41; 26:47; 13:13; 1 Chronicles 27:16-22; 2 Chronicles 30:11. Asher gave no judge, ruler, or hero to Israel. Anna is the most illustrious in this tribe's recorded history.

2. What other prophetesses does Scripture mention besides Anna? Exodus 15:20; Judges 4:4; Isaiah 8:3; 2 Kings 22:14; Acts 21:9; Nehemiah 6:14.

3. "The role of women in the life of our Lord is more prominent in the Gospel of Luke than in the other Gospels," declares Frances Vander Velde. She also calls Luke "the Woman's Gospel." [17] Study the 24 chapters of Luke to see if you agree. Make a list of women mentioned in Luke. What conclusions can you draw from the stories he chooses to tell?

4. Search Psalm 119 for verses that give reasons for memorizing Scripture. Can you find at least one verse for each of the five reasons cited in this chapter? Are there other reasons?

## GROUP DISCOVERIES

1. Divide into groups of three to five. Have all groups stand. At a signal, each group recites as many Bible verses as they can from memory. They may not look up any texts. No verse may be

repeated. Go round-robin style, each woman reciting one verse only when it is her turn. When the group runs out of verses, they should sit down. See which group can go the longest. You may have to call time on this one.

2. Discuss the suggestions for memorization given in this chapter. Which ones have those in the group tried? What works best for them? Do they have other ideas to suggest?

3. Share about a time when a verse of Scripture came to mind just when you needed it.

[1] Karl and Debbie Dortzbach, *Kidnapped* (New York: Harper and Row, 1975), pp. 4, 5, 36, 37, 92-95.

[2] E. G. White, *The Great Controversy,* pp. 593, 594.

[3] *Ibid.*, p. 600.

[4] R. Otis, ed., *A Gift of Love* (Hagerstown, Md.: Review and Herald Publishing Assn., 1994), p. 154.

[5] White, *The Great Controversy,* p. 600.

[6] Julie A. Talerico, "Elizabeth Mittelstaedt: Influencing a Nation," *Today's Christian Woman,* January/February 1992.

[7] J. Blackburn, *Roads to Reality,* pp. 112-117.

[8] E. G. White, *Counsels on Sabbath School Work* (Washington, D.C.: Review and Herald Publishing Assn., 1938), p. 42.

[9] A. Spangler and C. Turner, eds., *Heroes,* pp. 113-127.

[10] E. G. White, *Messages to Young People* (Washington, D.C.: Review and Herald Publishing Assn., 1930), p. 69.

[11] Paul Brand and Philip Yancey, *Pain: The Gift Nobody Wants* (Grand Rapids: HarperCollins, 1995), pp. 105, 106; Spangler and Turner, pp. 203-221; Dorothy Eaton Watts, *Stepping-Stones* (Hagerstown, Md.: Review and Herald, 1987), p. 370.

[12] Florence Littauer, *It Takes So Little to Be Above Average* (Eugene, Oreg.: Harvest House Publishers, 1983), p. 79.

[13] Ellen G. White, *Counsels to Parents, Teachers, and Students* (Mountain View, Calif.: Pacific Press Publishing Assn., 1913), pp. 137, 138.

[14] ———, *Education,* p. 42.

[15] *Ibid.*, p. 167.

[16] Darlene D. Rose, *Evidence Not Seen* (San Francisco: HarperCollins, 1990), pp. 170, 171.

[17] Frances Vander Velde, *Women of the Bible* (Grand Rapids.: Kregel Publications, 1957), p. 158.

16

# Facing
# the Flames

Those who pursue His presence will discover that it often leads them through fire. Sometimes the heat is symbolic, but for Joan Waste, a blind woman in Derby, England, the fire was real.

A convert to the Protestant faith, Joan desired the Word of God more than her necessary food. Although very poor, she saved until she had enough money for a New Testament. Then she scrimped some more to pay an old man to read to her daily.

Joan loved those times with The Word! She set about to memorize the parts she loved the most, and in time could repeat whole chapters by heart.

When Joan refused to attend the state church, the authorities charged her with heresy. "How do you answer this charge?" the local bishop asked.

"I believe exactly what the Bible teaches me," she spoke with quiet confidence. "If you can show me from the Scriptures the truth of what you want me to confess, then I will do it."

"You must answer for yourself," the bishop replied sternly. "Will you give up your beliefs or not?"

"No, sir, I cannot," Joan affirmed. "I will not forsake the truth of Scripture."

Sentenced to death, she was handed over to the sheriff. On August 1, 1556, the authorities led her to the stake. She knelt in a moment of prayer, then faced the flames courageously.[1]

## PERSECUTION AND TRIAL CAN BE EXPECTED

"It's time we freed ourselves from the prevalent idea that the power of God in a human life should lift it above all trials and conflicts," writes Ranelda Mack Hunsicker in *The Hidden Price of Greatness.*[2] We can expect the flames!

"The servant is not greater than his Lord," Jesus said. "If they have persecuted me, they will also persecute you." Paul emphasized the same truth: "All that will live godly in Christ Jesus shall suffer persecution" (1 Tim. 3:12).

Those women who have been serious in their pursuit of the presence of Christ in the Written Word have found courage to face the flames. Books could be filled with stories of brave women of the Word in recent times, for there are still countries in the world in which God's Word is cherished by few, scorned by many.

I was moved to tears at the 1995 General Conference session in Utrecht when 90-year-old Meropi Gjika of Albania gave her testimony. She evaded the secret police for 46 years in order to obey God's Word. In a cookie container she regularly placed a tithe of her meager income. When she handed it over to the first Adventist minister she met, it totaled $533.89. What courage it took for her to desire God's Word, to treasure it above all else![3]

Another courageous woman at the 1995 session was Evangelina Romanov. For many years she blanketed windows and her typing table to keep down the noise of typing forbidden devotional books, Sabbath school quarterlies, and Ellen G. White books. She struggled to procure typing paper and carbon paper without arousing the authorities.[4] Why did she and her husband risk imprisonment to publish these materials? The answer can be only that they treasured God's Word above all else, more than their freedom, more than their lives!

## COURAGE FOR THE FLAMES

It is God's Word alone that gives women courage in times of persecution. Women who have studied God's Word, believed its promises, and desired it above all else have become women willing to pursue God's presence through the fire.

Joyce Lewis, of Warwickshire, England, is an example of a woman with courage to face the flames. She had little desire for the Word until she witnessed the burning of Laurence Saunders.

"What terrible thing has this man done?" she inquired.

"He won't attend the Mass," someone replied. "He's one of those rogues who think they have to follow the Bible and the Bible only."

Curious, Joyce asked one of them to explain his beliefs.

"I advise you to study the Bible," the man replied. "Regulate your life and conduct by that alone."

Joyce got a Bible and began to read it for herself. Every spare moment she spent with the Word. It stirred her as nothing had ever done before. The more she studied, the more certain she became that she must follow God's Word, and that alone.

As a result the authorities brought Joyce before the bishop. "Why don't you participate in the rituals of the church?" he asked.

"I have not found those things in God's Word," she declared. "If they were commanded, I would receive them with all my heart."

"If you insist on believing only the Scripture, then you are a heretic," the bishop pronounced. He had Joyce imprisoned.

On the morning of her execution, the sheriff came to her cell where she had spent the night praying with friends. "Mrs. Lewis, I bring you tidings of the queen's command," he said. "You have but one hour more to live in this world—therefore prepare yourself!"

"Master Sheriff, your message is welcome to me," she replied. "I thank God that He has thought me worthy to venture my life in His cause."

When the fire was lit, Joyce lifted her hands to heaven, unafraid to follow her Lord even into the flames. Those who witnessed the scene testified that the presence of Christ was with her until the end.[5]

END-TIME PERSECUTION

Speaking of the persecution God's people will endure in the last days, Ellen White writes: "Their affliction is great, the flames of the furnace seem about to consume them; but the Refiner will bring them forth as gold tried in the fire. God's love for His children during the period of their severest trial is as strong and tender as in the days of their sunniest prosperity; but it is needful for them to be placed in the furnace of fire; their earthliness must be consumed, that the image of Christ may be perfectly reflected."[6]

Will you and I have the true courage of women of the Word to stand during our own time in the furnace, whether it be now or in the end-time? "All who will lay hold of God's promises . . . will succeed," we are promised.[7]

"We should now acquaint ourselves with God by proving His promises. . . . We must take time to pray."[8] Each of us must take time now to pursue God's presence in the Word so that we might have the courage to pursue Him in the fire.

### CLING TO THE WORD

Margaret of Scotland is one more example of a woman who did not shrink when the pursuit of God's presence led her to prison.

Guarded by soldiers, she was permitted out of prison to watch the death of Mrs. Lauchlison, a fellow Covenanter who insisted on obeying Scripture rather than the king's religion. The soldiers led her to the beach, where a wooden stake stood at the water's edge.

Margaret watched as they bound her friend to a wooden pole. She stared as the tide came in, slowly raising the water level about the woman tied to the stake. Each wave brought the water higher about her body.

"What has the old woman done?" someone cried out of the crowd.

"She was found on her knees in prayer," a guard answered.

As Margaret kept staring at her friend, the old woman's wrinkled face seemed aglow with heavenly light. Margaret strained to catch her words above the crash of the waves. "I have promised to obey Thee, heavenly Father. Help me now when I am tested."

The faint strains of a hymn sounded above the pounding waves. Margaret watched as they washed over the old woman's head. *Lord, help me to be as faithful to Your Word,* she breathed a silent prayer of commitment.

The next day Margaret was the one tied to the stake. As the tide came in she quoted words that were dearer to her than life: "If God be for us, who can be against us? Who can divide us from the love of Christ? Not height or depth, nor any other creature."[9]

*Lord, You are dearer to me than all else in this world. Your Word*

*is of more value than silver and gold. Keep me faithful to Your Word.*
*Help me to be willing to pursue Your presence, even through the fire.*

Search the Word

## Loyal Priscilla

References: Acts 18:2, 18, 26; Romans 16:3-5; 1 Corinthians 16:19; 2 Timothy 4:19; *The Acts of the Apostles,* pp. 243-258.

"One of the most influential women in the New Testament Church was Priscilla, a Jewess who had come out of Italy with her husband Aquila, to live first at Corinth and about eighteen months later at Ephesus. They had left Rome at the time when Claudius, in his cruel and unjust edict, had expelled all Jews." [10]

"Priscilla . . . was not afraid to sacrifice for the cause of Christ. She lived in a day of great prejudice and opposition to the Christ of the Christian Church. She confessed Christ in a day when Christians faced great persecution. But Priscilla was not afraid, even if it might cost her her life." [11]

1. **Observation**
   a. What can you discover about Priscilla's career, marriage, leadership ability, hospitality, adaptability, loyalty, status in the church, friendship with Paul, places she lived and worked? Jot down the facts.
   b. On Bible maps locate each place mentioned.
   c. Where and when do you think Priscilla risked her life for Paul? (Acts 18:12; 19:29, 30)
2. **Interpretation**
   a. Write a brief character sketch of Priscilla.
   b. Notice the position of Priscilla's name in several of the passages. It goes against the culture of the day. What does it suggest about Paul's attitude toward women?
   c. Apollos was a learned scholar with whom Priscilla reasoned about the gospel. What does this tell you about her abilities and the view of the early church toward women?
   d. Why do you think Paul included information about Priscilla in his writings?
   e. What indications do you have that Priscilla truly desired the Word?
   f. "According to tradition Priscilla died a martyr's death." [12]

What indication do you find that Priscilla was courageous enough to face the fires of persecution?

3. Application
   a. If Priscilla spent a week in your home, what do you think would disturb her most? What would she appreciate?
   b. Imagine that Priscilla writes you after spending time in your home. What do you think she would say to you?

PERSONAL DISCOVERIES

1. A Bible dictionary or a concordance will give you interesting details as to the meaning of Priscilla's name and possible reasons that Paul often mentions her name first. Also, you may find nonbiblical references to Priscilla and her literary accomplishments as well as her martyrdom. You can learn more about her trade. What other interesting facts can you discover?

2. Do a word study of the words "persecute" and "persecution." From your study, make a summary statement about what the Bible teaches about the persecution of those who pursue God's presence.

3. Make a collection of Bible promises for those who face the flames of trial and persecution because of their beliefs.

GROUP DISCOVERIES

1. What do you most admire about Priscilla? Why? Let all who are willing share their personal response to Priscilla as a person.

2. Brainstorm about courageous women of the Bible. What other women do you think had the courage to face the flames because of their devotion to God and His Word?

3. How has this Bible study series affected your life?

4. Ask the group to think of women they know who have made great sacrifices to follow God's Word. Has the group read any stories of any modern women who have pursued the presence of God even into the fires of persecution?

[1] John Foxe, *Christian Martyrs of the World* (Westwood, N.J.: Barbour, 1985), pp. 521, 522.

[2] Ray Beeson and Ranelda Mack Hunsicker, *The Hidden Price of Greatness* (Wheaton, Ill.: Tyndale House Publishers, Inc., 1991), p. xiv.

[3] *Adventist Review,* July 3, 1995.

[4] Nancy J. Vymeister, "A Story of Courage and Sacrifice," *Adventist Review,* July 6, 1995.

[5] Foxe, pp. 542-546.

[6] E. G. White, *The Great Controversy,* p. 621.

[7] *Ibid.*

[8] *Ibid.*, p. 622.

[9] Glenna Barstad, *They Dared for God* (Boise, Idaho: Pacific Press Publishing Assn., 1958), pp. 80-84.

[10] Edith Deen, *All of the Women of the Bible* (New York: Harper and Row, 1955), p. 227.

[11] F. Vander Velde, *Women of the Bible,* p. 249.

[12] *Ibid.*

# On Wings of Praise

## by Kay D. Rizzo

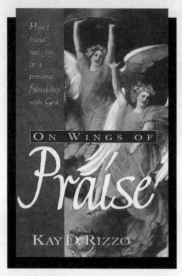

K ay Rizzo shares how praise to God lifted her from her "spiritual winter" and filled her life with a joy and power she had never known. "I discovered that praise was a *choice*, not a response," Rizzo writes. And her conscious decision to praise God in all things had a profound effect on both her personal and spiritual life. "Prayer combined with praise changed my heart," Rizzo says. "It will change yours, too." In this upbeat book she shows you how.

Paper, 171 pages.
US$12.99, Cdn$18.99.